1

CHRONICLES
OF A WORN SOUL

"On the path
of understanding"

To my *brothers*,

Hank, Bruce and Pat

All better men than me
I miss them

Preface

Being raised in the Church of Jesus Christ of Latter-Day Saints, I am honored to say that I have been blessed with many opportunities to serve in the Kingdom. I have held nearly every possible position short of General Authority that can be held by an Aaronic and Melchizedek Priesthood holder and some of them multiple times. They include callings as Deacons Quorum President, Elders Quorum President, Branch President, Bishop and Counselor in the Stake Presidency.

Many other stake and ward positions have come my way and has offered me a distinctive view of the workings of the church and its collective doctrine. This experience gives me a unique prospective from the "grass roots" as a lay minister and has offered me the insight I need to make sense of my life and those I have been called to counsel.

My counseling approach is direct and "to-the-point." As a result, I have offended many people through the years who prefer a more gentle hand. I love the Lord and *want* to be gentle and would never want to offend anyone. However, there comes a time when we need to say what is needed, right?

Members of the Church are just like everyone else. They are not exempt from the challenges of the world and many of them make the same foolish decisions that others make. The big difference is that they have the restored gospel of Jesus Christ and the constant companion of the Holy Ghost to guide them. Sadly, in many cases, these great and special resources elude their attention and they fall into the same traps that Satan sets for the children of men. Though physically mature, many operate on the intellectual deductive level of a child while others become so confused by the "dust of life"[1] they cannot see the path before them.

My four year old grandson Tucker was recently struggling to keep up with me on a nature trail in Southern Virginia. "Pops stop," he demanded. I promptly replied, "No Tucker, we must keep moving. People are just like sharks, they must keep moving forward or they will die."

To me, this little "tongue in cheek" exchange exemplifies a much greater meaning in life. Many of us keep moving but the direction is questionable. If we stop, we will cease motion and therefore progression. Further, many of us engage in motion without understanding our objective, destination or even our purpose.

As each of us move along the path of life, we struggle to understand if we are being pushed, pulled or dragged. Some fail to understand if they are the subject of the forces of motion or if they are the forces themselves.

The stories presented in the following pages represent my walk upon the path of life in search for understanding of these and many other questions. Our Father in Heaven created things to "act and things to be

---

[1] A message from the Dust... of Life: Chapter 23

acted upon."[2] By virtue of your presence in this study it is obvious that you seek wisdom and understanding and wish to be the one to act (proactionary) rather than the one to be acted upon (reactionary).

We will walk together from childhood, to maturity using the experiences of life in search of understanding. Many of these stories and experiences will relate to similar ones in your own life.

I am confident that as you turn the last page of this book, you will have a greater level of insight and understanding on why and how the events in your life came to be and how they have affected you as the Lord shapes and mold us to be instruments in His hand.

On the trail of life, my sole is worn (as are yours). Rather than looking back on the scenery passed as obstacles, I pray that we can see them as "lessons along the way." These Chronicles therefore, should serve us well, *on the path of understanding.*

---

[2] 2 Nephi 2:14

Contents

SECTION V: AS UNDERSTANDING BECOMES <u>CERTAINITY</u>

"Dealing with the more complex issues"

SECTION VI: THINGS BECOME CLEAR AS WE LOOK BACK, <u>ETERNAL TRUTH...</u>......287

"Life is a process of understanding."

SECTION 1

**The simple truths
Of
Basic understanding
Dealt
With as a child**

Let's begin by discussing some of the most basic levels of understanding faced by children. Let's understand what they must be overcome before they can progress.

Truth, Basic #1: We come from the throne of God, He is our Father.

IN THE END, IT IS HE AND I

As a small boy, I would look outside myself to imagine what kind of man I would turn out to be. What would I accomplish, who would I become and what would my life be like? As a child, all of the questions that can be asked stream in front of our minds eye as a ticker tape from the New York Stock Exchange.

Our lives are being defined on a daily basis as we make decisions that will mold and shape who we are and who we will become. Though we are placed in the ruts formed by our guardians, we waddle along its grooved path forward bouncing off the edges from time to time as a pinewood derby car plummeting ever forward into our future.

As we acquire bits of knowledge, we focus on those parental faces above us who look down to provide examples regardless of their intentions. As our small minds implant the behavior into our own developing thought processors, we make judgments of right and wrong, good or bad and how these observations apply to us.

Over time, the accumulated observations develop patterns of behavior that define our own behavior. In other words, we become a product of our environment.

To *equalize* these mental inputs, the Lord has given us the ability to filter them through our spiritual self, our conscious. *"And the spirit givith light to every man that cometh into the world; and the Spirit enlighteth every man through the world that harkeneth to the voice of the spirit."*[3] This point is again mentioned in the Book of Mormon,

> *"For behold, the spirit of Christ is given to every man, that he may know good from evil: wherefore, I show unto you the way to judge; for every thing which inviteth to do good, and to persuade to believe in Christ, is sent forth by the power and gift of Christ; wherefore ye may know with a perfect knowledge it is of God."*[4]

---

[3] D&C 84:46
[4] Moroni 7:16

No man is left alone, ever. The years that occupied my childhood were not happy ones. As I fell victim to violent strokes of a strict disciplinarian father, I would seek solace from an imaginary friend that had no face or physical form but was there still the same. I could feel His presence in the quiet places outside the home; mostly in the woods.

I would go there often to seek the peace I found in that place and dilute the painful images of a confused family with the peace and calm of the natural things of the earth. There was a presence there that I could not define at first but later recognized it as the same presence I felt when performing my duties as a Deacon. It was a presence that brought me closer to the spirit within me that drew its strength from above the lofty tops of the forest and even into the stars and beyond.

Examples were always an important part of my personal development. I would identify and follow those who I observed I would want to be like. They were good examples for me to follow, I thought. One by one, they all eventually fell from the perch of acceptability into the depository of past heros. The succession progressed along the tracks of life until, as an adult, I made an important realization. There was only one mortal man that ever lived that was without flaw, Jesus Christ

Mortality is filled with brutality from every direction. It is Satan's way. As those that follow Him pursue their ambitions, those that stand in their way suffer.

Many times in my life, I have felt alone. Through acts of rejection, betrayal, neglect or oversight, I have felt abandoned by friends, family or associates. As with all of us, we experience these situations in all aspects of life to include work, family and church. It is in those places we consider holy that such offenses seem to have the most damaging effect. The usual consequence is inactivity or apostasy from the church. This is not an option however, when you know the Gospel is true.

On the many occasions that I have faced this circumstance, I have reverted to my childhood and sought solace "in the woods." This term becomes figurative at times as I seek the spirit I felt in those quiet places where I felt His spirit. It eventually became the one retreat that was forever and faithfully waiting for my return. This is where I found God, the never changing example of goodness that was constant, deliberate, stable and absolutely faithful to me in my pleadings for peace.

No matter when or where I am hurt physically, emotionally or spiritually, He is always there. I have come to understand that truth as a guiding principle of my life. It is truth that applies to each and every one of us on earth. Distinctive beings but one in purpose, He is our Father, Our Savior and the Holy Spirit that accompanies each of us in all things so long as we *"harken to the voice of the spirit."*[5]

Many of our youth follow the temptations of peers to enter into the dark recesses of human behavior. As I faced these decisions as a youth, I would hear the still small voice I recognized from "the woods" giving direction because I knew that God could not go to the place I was tempted to go. There, I would be without my friend and truly be left alone; a reality I could not imagine.

It is the love of this spiritual presence that kept me from the frivolities of life as a youth to the present day. Having experienced the pains associated with conflict of life, I knew that without this *friend* I could not bear to face the challenges of life without Him. It is this deeply personal relationship with this eternal spirit that has kept me drawing closer to Him because I realized that in the end, it is He and I.

The problem is that the voices drawing us to earthly matters are louder than that little voice within. They capture the hearts and minds of our youth all too frequently.

Pain is the condition that seeks a remedy. Is it only when we feel pain of the spirit that we seek God? Sadly, this is more true than not but seek God we must. Inevitably, poor judgment brings pain and suffering of some variety. We must seek truth before our mistakes demand a realignment of our lives.

Many of our youth grow to become missionaries, husbands, fathers and mothers without having to seek these

---

[5] D&C 84:46

truths. There was no reason to; they have been protected from the world by family, church and neighbors. Although this is an admirable condition, it can have unintended consequences. Having never been *pushed* their spiritual muscles will not develop; they never had to!

My early life is not a good example for anyone; however, in the midst of the family conflict, I came to know God and the Holy Ghost that delivers His spirit. As my parents would fight, I felt His spirit saying, "It will be OK. I am here." As I heard discouraging words coming from my beloved parent seeking to steer me away from the church, I felt the presence of my friend saying, "It is ok. I am here."

It was once my opportunity to sit at the desk of a Bishop who felt it appropriate to outline my many faults. His observations were made regarding a conflict emerging in the ward to which he held me responsible. His information was faulty and ill-advised but I faced the reprisal respectfully. It was later that I felt betrayed and abandoned by those I felt to esteem but within I felt the calming spirit of my dearest friend; again I realized that in the end, it is He and I.

As the years pass as pickets on the fence on the high speed freeway of life, we may feel alone many times to face the endless trials of life. However, with these trials come cumulative experiences and wisdom in the knowledge that among them all comes one constant, a divine presence staying ever closer to our spirit bring us comfort in our darkest hours.

With all that we have come to learn and know in mortality, one thing is as certain to me as the sun, wind, stars and moon; in the end, it will be He and I. Along with this knowledge comes the understanding that where He is, will be His Gospel. Where His Gospel is, will be my family, my faith and my eternal blessings. With this understanding comes the comforting knowledge that nothing else really matters; only that small but eternal one on one relationship that keeps us going no matter what; He and I.

Truth, Basic #2:

Children are selfish.

I WANT IT NOW!
(Today's pottage)

They have to be. They understand that they must be fed or they will be hungry. They understand that they are dependent on the caregiver and that they have no control to take care of themselves. Some of us never progress beyond this instinct.

It is early in the history of mankind that we see examples of those who do not understand the precious things in our lives. In this Old Testament story of Jacob and Esau, we learn of a *man of the world* (Esau) who did not understanding spiritual matters. Jacob offered his brother a bowl of pottage *(oatmeal)* for his birthright. Esau was hungry. By all definitions this is a perfect example of being "short sighted."

Under the patriarchal order in force during that period of time, the birthright was the right to inheritance including land and the authority to preside. The firstborn of flocks and of human families was considered as belonging to the Lord and was expected to be dedicated to him.[6] It was however a *right* and not an *obligation.* As is most opportunities to serve the Lord, it is a matter of choice and not a requirement.

> *"And Jacob s sod pottage: and Esau came from the field, and he was faint. And Esau said sell me this day thy birthright. And Esau said, Behold I am at the point to die: and what profit shall this birthright do to me?"* [7]

Esau gave up the most valued right of his life for instant gratification of no lasting value or purpose. Because Esau was ruled by the world (physical) he had no value in spiritual things (spiritual). The tradeoff was immeasurably against Esau but he agreed all the same. Although the thought seems preposterous at face value, we see all around us the perpetuation of this principle continually in our everyday lives.

It is interesting to see how different people deal with things considered precious. We are told by the Lord that there are things we are given that are considered precious and sacred to be valued above our lives. They are

---

[6] Bible Dictionary
[7] Genesis 25:29-32

received in the temple. They have no value in and of themselves but our charge to maintain their precious standing is the basis for how we will be judged.

Here is an example. I hold out a stone and give it to you with the charge that it is the most precious stone on the earth. You are to guard it with your life because "I" said so. If you value me and my word, you will do as I have asked. If you *"esteem them as things of naught"*[8] it will be of no value to you and a direct reflection on the degree of reverence you hold toward me and my *precious* object.

The value of the stone is immaterial; its value is based on your perception of who you are entrusting it for. What if it was the Lord Himself who gave you the stone? Would your interest in its safekeeping be different? Your treatment of the stone is a direct representation of your reverence for the giver.

In the words of the apostle Matthew, we hear of the servants being given talents.[9] The Lord gives each of us talents (precious things). These talents come from the creator and are by definition given to us as an inheritance. At times it would appear that the talents of others seem to outnumber our own. Some talents we recognize develop and grow into a skill or ability. Others, we ignore and leave them to drift into oblivion. What do we do with the talents we do not care about? Are they buried...or multiplied?

---

[8] 2 Nephi 33:5-9
[9] St Matthew 25

We can use these God given talents for various purposes according to our *agency*. Our society is trained in the art of instant gratification, *do not wait, get it now*. This is the seed sewn in the fabric of our society as families are defined as the culture sees fit. There are no rules and no standards. There is no "benefit" in waiting for anything.

This precept runs counter to God's eternal plan. We live this life through restraint and discipline to standards set to obtain an eternal reward in the life to come. Therefore it is easy to understand how this *get it now standard* is based in worldly precepts. *"For the natural man is an enemy to God."*[10]

Many of us give up eternal blessings associated with our birthright for the "get it now" world. We hunger for fine apparel, luxuries of life, fame and lusts. As a result, we trade our birthright. Through the indulgence in these conditions, we give up what we could have become.

Recently, I had an opportunity to counsel with a good, faithful sister who wishes she could change her past. In her mid-fifties, this otherwise composed sister fought to hold back the tears as she recalled a time in her earlier life when she received her patriarchal blessing. It promised her temple blessings associated with an eternal marriage to a fine worthy young man. Children would come into her home that would be a "blessing to her, every day of her life." There was a young man on his mission that was faithful in writing her.

---

[10] Mosiah 3:19

On his return, he sought after her but she turned him away as her youthful interest remained on the things of the world. Eventually, he lost interest and found another. As she grew older and matured she looked back with regret and wished she had been more mature to recognize the humble goodness in his character but lacked the *glitter* the world had taught her to look for in a suitor .

Having never found the boy to fit her romantic profile, she grew older and wanted to get married and start a family. She married a non-member who later joined but with lackluster interest in the church and his priesthood responsibilities. She struggled to hold back the tears as she confided how hard it is to love the man who has fallen so short of her earlier expectation. She constantly reminds herself of "what might have been" if she had remained faithful in her choices so that the blessings promised decades earlier in her blessing could have been realized.

Silently, my heart was breaking as I have heard this story over and over again as I have been called to serve Gods children. Truly "of all the words of tongue or pen, the saddest of these, what might have been."[11] Her birthright of temple marriage was sold for the frivolity of youth.

After reading the story of Jacob and Esau, it is natural to accuse Esau of foolishness to trade so much for so little. It may be more difficult to believe that we may do it ourselves every day. We trade accomplishment and success for laziness and apathy. We trade the joy of an

---

[11] John Greenleaf Whittier 1807-1892

eternal family for instant gratification through lust or infidelity. We trade our health and mental capabilities for drugs, alcohol and other stimulants. We trade precious time we could have with spouse and children as we extend our work hours into the evenings and weekends for fancy cars, homes and assorted recreational luxuries. We trade our souls for the riches of the world and the fame and notoriety that come with a celebrity status. After these considerations, it is not so difficult to see how such a thing can happen.

The greatest treasures are usually received after paying the highest price. The same is true with spiritual things. The greatest gifts we can acquire in this life and in the life to come are spiritually based for all things are spiritual unto the Lord.[12]

Pottage is a simple bowl of physical sustenance that will satisfy an immediate physical urge that can never be eliminated until the body ceases to exist. Hunger is a trial. It is through overcoming physical trials by placing the will of the mind firmly in control over the urges of the body that greater ideals can be accomplished.

Trials come in many forms, physical, emotional and spiritual. The prospect of *"eat drink and be merry for tomorrow we die"* [13] is alive and well in societies moral fabric. We must ask ourselves the question. "Is this what we want for ourselves?' How many of us have traded our birthrights for the pottage of the world?

---

[12] D&C 29:34
[13] 2 Nephi 28:8

It was Satan's plan to trade a lot (agency) for compulsion (a little). It was Christ's plan to trade exaltation (a lot), for a little (obedience). In both cases the trade is not fair. Immeasurable worth is being traded for something of insignificance by comparison.

In actuality, all that we see, feel and touch on this earth belongs to God. He made it and allowed us to use it for His purposes. There is nothing that we can give him that He does not already own. Our thoughts and actions are the only thing that truly belongs to us. It is all that we can give. Why then is this decision of obedience so hard for many to make? The choice seems simple but we see these absurd choices made every day.

Many will trade the eternal blessings of the Temple because they refuse to obey the law of tithing or the word of wisdom. The motive is selfishness, *potage*. There are those who deny themselves the blessings of the gospel in their own and in their families' lives because someone has offended them. The basis of this is pride. Pride is another example of trading a birthright for pottage.

I am sure that in our preexistent state it was hard for any of us to conceive how we would choose the world over our eternal home. Its examples are all around us and perhaps in our own lives. We need to constantly look at the choices we make in our lives and consider what choices we are making; hopefully, we are wise in the process. Skip the potage and go for the *bread of life*.[14] Don't give away your eternity for a few "right nows."

---

[14] John 6:35

Truth, Basic #3:
    Children follow examples

HEROES?

As with most, I share in the feelings that to read is to become engaged in an adventure or to join in a quest of those who have performed or accomplished extraordinary things. We unite with them as they scale the tallest peaks, journey beyond our imagination and accomplish amazing feats. In the process we enter another world, one outside of our own. We see the world through their eyes and feel what they feel. In a small sense, this temporary respite from the emotional challenges of life, we are allowed an escape from our reality and be "someone special."

    Somehow, in the magic strokes of the writer's pen, we become immersed in "their" world and suddenly realize, their life is better than ours. We imagine that they do not have to face the things we do and if they did, they would be more capable and creative than we. As the last page of the vicarious journey is turned however, we look up to face the same life issues we faced on page one. It is this illusion that drives us to the bookstores, movie theaters, athletic fields and concert halls by the millions to receive entertainment. We must be entertained, right? Those employed by this industry internalize this praise as if they themselves are joyfully responsible for our happiness. As a result, their personal behavior is beyond any potential reproach by their adorning followers. Their "hero" status is solely based on their ability as an actor, athlete or celebrity.

Where is the meaningful basis for the status we have awarded them? Especially when they usually treat this respect with a tone of entitlement accompanied with the prideful glance from beneath a stiff neck and downward glare.

Certainly, they are not to blame. They did not demand the admiration graciously poured upon them. It was given to them freely. Those who profit from their celebrity build them up to be larger than life. To access their valuable presence we must pay the price of admission or purchase the product they promote. After all, is not a bad thing to have heroes, right? It is important, if not essential, to have good examples in our lives. However, herein lays the fundamental problem: who should they be?

Growing up, I knew that I needed to look outside my home for the appropriate "role model." Even as a child, it is easy to recognize the difference as discipline ventures into the realm of abuse. Trying to establish a path of life that would lead me to who I wanted to become, I knew that the example would have to come from outside my family.

One by one, they fell short of my expectation. As the years passed, I realized that in the end, I was to become whoever I wanted to be. It was my decisions and choices that would create my character and personality. There is comfort in this understanding but it provides little direction for a searching child that needs good examples. Again, the question lingers, where are they to be found?

There is only so much that a parent can do. Either at infancy or in adulthood, the young will eventually have to face those that would destroy them. This threat can come in many forms and in many cases are disguised as friends. In fact, the friends may consider themselves as just that: friends, when in fact their destructive influences bring both (themselves and their *friends*) to the door of the destroyer. These friends may be the same "heroes" they have identified in their lives.

Recognizing the difference from one to another can be challenging. In many cases, the facilitator of destruction represents the nurturer but later transforms into something else; something sinister. The trust once gained, is more difficult to dispel than if trust had never been gained. This truly gives advantages to the forces of nature that would cause us harm.

The problem is that our judgments on these matters are filtered by the "way things are in the world."

As a result, the examples we search for should be one of ideals, values and principles. In these instances, our examples become easier to find. They are found in the child's bedroom reading stories before naps, behind the wheel of the family sedan driving to soccer practice and in the homes of those they can influence for good.

They are those who personally affect the lives of people for good in the professions, vocations and classrooms in life. They are those who stand up for what they believe in, in all walks of life. They are they who live the life they project without pretense or disguise.

Heroes are becoming harder and harder to find in a day where there are debates regarding the unbridled levels of behavior itself. At some point in our lives, each of us needs to set a standard for personal behavior. In this process we need to consider where this behavior will lead us and what we will become.

At some point, our attention turns from our search for a hero to the possibility of becoming one ourselves. It may not be our intention or something that we are comfortable but one day, we may attract the interest of another who they would like to emulate, then the tables turn add the responsibility upon our shoulders to assure that we will never do anything to become the fallen heroes of our past.

As I acknowledge my advancing years, I have come to one very well informed decision: there is one person that can always be used as an example. One that will never turn away or disappoint; it is the Savior, Himself. He walked among us, walked, talked, drank laughed and cried. I understood that He would be the only one that would never let me down and one to which I could always depend on.

I had plenty of plausible excuses to misbehave as a youth; I had plenty of bad examples. However, I knew that the Lord knew me and was aware of my circumstances. I felt as if He was the one that was always there to illuminate my exit from danger. It was a personal relationship that only I had with Him. I knew that I had no excuse that would *fly* with Him and I never wanted to disappoint Him. I have come to realize now more than ever, that is was my Savior that was my hero all along. He was, is and will always be the only one void of imperfection.

This should be our goal; to follow Him and be like Him in all that we do and say. This is the true Hero in our life and to the world, *"I am the light of the world: he that followeth me shall not walk in darkness, but shall have light of life."[15]*

---

[15] St. John 8:12

Truth, Basic #4:

We all have fears.

FEAR IS NOT NECESSARILY A BAD THING

"What is fear?" It was just a casual discussion among friends discussing the "signs of the times" associated with the Second Coming of Christ. There are many signs prophesized that have already taken place and others are yet to come. Is the Second Coming something to fear?

The definition of fear varies with people. To some, it is the feeling of anxiety caused by the presence of anticipated danger. To others, it is respect or awe for someone or something. For others, it is just plain worry. I have never met anyone that was not afraid. Each of us have our own fears. Some are rational and some are not but for each of us they are real.

It is this fear that sometimes drives us to accomplish great things. And for others it is the source of depression, fulfillment of self-fulfilling prophesy. It is in the fear of poverty that we spend countless hours in university libraries to study our professional disciplines. It is the fear of "second place" that we practice, train and push ourselves to the limits of endurance. It is the fear for our lives that we do things that we would otherwise never consider. The fear of human loss drives fire fighters into burning buildings and soldiers into harm's way. Fear is the term that defines much of who we are and what we become.

When we have no food, we fear starvation. When water is difficult to acquire, we fear dehydration. However, when we have an ample supply of each, we are no longer afraid.

Fear can also be associated with the lack of preparation. In connection with the Second Coming of Christ, some people fear because they are not prepared for it. However, we are told that, "If ye are prepared ye shall not fear?"[16] How does preparation dispel fear? The worst kind of fear lives in the spirit of the unknown. We fear things we do not understand. What lies beyond that corner, who lurks in the dark and what unknown calamity awaits in the uncertainty of the future?

How do we prepare for spiritual famine? The restored gospel of Jesus Christ tells us that there will never be a time that the Lord will not be accessible through prayers that give us personal revelation. Therefore, as we

---

[16] D&C 38:30

draw closer to Heavenly Father and invite His spirit into our lives, we feel His presence and influence that brings the comfort and peace. The status of peace is a state of mental calm free from anxiety; there is no room for fear.

Growing up, I was not the smallest guy in the class but there always seemed to be a larger kid that wanted to prove his superiority at my expense. Though I was always able to "hold my own" it became troublesome at times. I began to study martial arts in my late teens and continued through adulthood. As I prepared myself for self-defense, I no longer fear the potential need for using it. Preparation conquers fear.

It was through the fear of God that I kept myself in line as a youth. I was afraid of disappointing Him. I knew that He knew who I was and what I was thinking. I was afraid to offend Him. I knew I could not fool Him. It was fear that kept me in line. Is that a bad thing? Could fear, in this case be substituted for respect? To respect someone is to have a feeling of admiration. If you admire someone and care what they think of you, would you not behave in a way that would please them?

At an early age, we are taught the plan of salvation in Primary. The training continues in the youth programs, the mission field and the Temples. After grasping the concepts of these lifelong principles, where is there room for fear?

Certainly, there will be fear associated with our lack of worthiness to face God. In this case, fear works to our advantage. Fear becomes an instrument to correct our path and precipitate our repentance. If we know that preparation is essential, we fear for the fate of those we love and are not prepared. It is therefore also knowledge for the need to prepare that dispels fear and keeps us on the straight and narrow path.

I have had instances in my life when I have stood at the threshold of mortality. As I matured, there was no fear when considering the possibility of death. Because of my understanding of the transition between the spiritual realities of earth and the eternal realm, there was no unknown factor. I knew what awaited me and who I would know there. I have friends there that I would love to see again.

There are many who do not fully embrace the truths of the Gospel in and outside the church. Because they fear their ability to maintain the disciplined lifestyle, they reject the teachings and fall into a state of being unprepared. Now demands are lifted, freeing their agenda for more entertaining activities.

The fear of being wrong drives many to hostility toward the church and its message. These are those who may pursue a path to derail the work as did Alma the younger.[17] In this pursuit, they will no longer be burdened with the demand for obedience and thereby be relieved of the fear of the truth.

In a very real way, this tactic describes the modern day tactics of the Adversary. He will attack truth by whatever method necessary to turn away the hearts of the children of man leaving them unprepared to meet God. This

---

[17] Alma 27:32

reality is the fear that drives many missionaries across the world to warn their neighbor.[18] This is the fear that the mother has for her wayward son and the priesthood leader has for his quorum who falls short in the pursuit of righteousness.

Used in the hands of the Lord, fear is transformed to represent love, respect and honor. As we serve Him we would fear behavior that would cause His absence thus denying us the blessings associated with obedience. The prepared have knowledge of the things to come and the consequences while the unknowledgeable or apathetic soul hurls toward harm.

This should be the real source of fear! *"Fear not them which kill the body, but are not able to kill the soul: but rather fear him which is able to destroy both soul and body in hell."*[19]

It is prophesized in the Doctrine and Covenants when speaking of the second coming of Christ that, *"...all things shall be in commotion and surely, men's hearts shall fail them, for fear shall come upon all people."*[20] What does it mean for the "hearts of men to fail them?" This condition would be associated with fear taken to an extreme level we know as panic.

The word panic is associated with other words of similar meaning such as fright, terror, dread, alarm and horror. These words do not describe anyone I know (under any circumstance) who truly understands who they are as a

---

[18] D&C 88:81
[19] Matt 10:28
[20] D&C 88:91

faithful and knowledgeable child of God. Death may bring disappointment that they will not be able to continue association with their loved ones but none of those words would describe their mental condition as they faced the calamities of the earth. In contrast, I can imagine these good people saying, "Well, here we go. It has begun."

We know what will happen on the earth in the latter days. It is prophesized. There will be trouble and lots of it. Those who are prepared do not fear it. They have knowledge of the doctrine and have faith in the Leadership in the Kingdom. The Lord has placed them on the earth and called them by prophesy. He has promised us that our Prophet shall never lead us astray.

Those who have knowledge shall not fear. Rather than running for the figurate hills, and engaging in fear and panic, the prepared among us will simply say, "Bring it on!"

There are many who choose to be unprepared. It is simply too much trouble. "I know that it will happen. I just don't have the time to prepare, and besides, if I need something, my neighbor has it." Although sadly familiar, this outlines the situation of the ten virgins.[21]

If there is room for fear in our lives, it should only be associated with the fear of ignorance. It is important that we learn all that we can to understand how we need to be prepared for any spiritual calamity that may arise. If there is to be fear in our hearts, it should be the fear of evil, disobedience and rebellion. This fear then becomes

---

[21] Matt 25:1

knowledge of what the consequences of these behaviors bring. Fear becomes knowledge, knowledge becomes preparation and preparation brings peace. It is as simple as that.

Truth, Basic #5:
We need to be taught
the appropriate use of the word "No."

NO, THANK YOU

A few years ago, my wife and I were on a car trip along with other tourist crossing the Sinai dessert from Cairo, Egypt to the ferries of the Red Sea. It was a scheduled six hour trip by car from our hotel to the ferries where we would continue our middle-eastern journey to Jordan and eventually to Jerusalem. In a fifteen passenger van, we were accompanied by a local driver, tour guide and a single heavily armed security agent.

Being a veteran, I recognized the weapon and knew that by its skillful use, it was capable of repelling anything but the most organized and coordinated threat. I passed it off as a display of concern for our safety and welfare by those responsible but dismissed the probability of its ultimate need. As we passed through each checkpoint, there was considerable discussion between our custodians and those manning the station. Sometimes voices were raised and aggressive arm movements accompanied their speech as our presence and destination were obviously being discussed. Being unable to understand the Arabic exchange, I trusted that our custodians were representing our best interest. This suspicion was confirmed multiple times as we progressed along this most desolate stretch of Gods earth.

Suffering from a condition of "hyper-vigilance" I was more attentive to our stressful progression than most as I felt the passion in the voices of those periodic questioners holding weapons of war on their shoulders and hips. After passing one such outpost we soon crested a hill where the vision of the road stretched unencumbered as it disappeared into the distant mountains.

A few miles ahead on the passenger side curb was a large object that later revealed itself as a passenger bus. As we approached, I could see that the windows were significantly tented to restrict any view of its interior. Beside it was a man in military uniform standing in the middle of the road attempting to hail our vehicle. Waving his hands in crossing fashion, it was obvious that he wanted us to stop, apparently to render assistance to a disabled vehicle.

Knowing the potential threat this situation represented, I sat up alertly watching for the reaction of our care-takers. As I was poised to voice an immediate and unmistakable opinion on the subject, the driver never hesitated in his resolve to continue at full speed ignoring pedestrian distracter. With the weapon of our security officer positioned in the "ready" mode, we speedily approached and passed the man with his sidearm awaiting orders.

As we rushed along the desolate, abandoned highway I looked back to see the man observing the quickly shrinking subject of his latest ambition. As my heart was racing over the possible change in our life status that was just avoided, I looked carefully at my fellow travelers going about their private individual pastimes oblivious to the averted peril.

The set up was a classic scenario where an apparent helpless and stranded traveler needed faithful assistance from a passing "good Samaritan." Once the forward motion had ceased, the neighboring bus (troop carrier) empties its human cargo, and the American tourist become international bargaining chips at the mercy of the overwhelming force. In an instant, life would have forever changed for us desert travelers.

Instead, the wise custodian understood his priorities, weighed the potential outcomes, leveled the "risk/reward" factors and simply said "No thank you" to those attempting to alter his course. In a seemingly innocent and legitimate situation, where honest curiosity could have weighed the decision, the benefit of "life experiences" ruled the decision making process which led to our safe delivery to the port of departure.

In later contemplation of the situation, I often wonder what would have happened if we had actually stopped as requested. The answer is simply and profoundly, "no telling" and that is the problem. This situation is actually quite reminiscent of many of our life's choices. We are joyfully traveling along the highway of life when we are hailed by a curious situation. In our mind we say, "This looks interesting let's stop and check it out."

When we do, it captures us in a most deadly grip that could forever change the course of our lives. It could be a pretty (handsome) face that we meet in a potentially dangerous place. Maybe a party that appeared to be curiously interesting. We knew at the time that something was not right, it just did not "fit" but we overlooked our "reason" developed through life's experiences and surrendered to the curiosity of the moment.

Once we stop and the bus empties to seal our fate, we are addicted to the drug, heavy with the child or responsible for the consequences of the small moment in our lives that will forever alter our course. From that time forward, the direction of our life's highway is diverted from its original trajectory. Try as we might to find our original course, our point of origin is diverted by miles, days, weeks or years.

Considering that pivotal point in our lives, many of us wish they could simply turn back the hands of time and as we approached that roadside bus simply say, "No thank you." In the defense of those among us who seek to do good, there is a "fine line" between pursuing that endeavor and endangering ourselves and /or our families.

Life experiences usually serve to make us wiser. It is this wisdom that filters what we see through what we know. When something seems "out of place" or just doesn't "feel right" it usually sends up warning signs that we should pay particular attention to. It is when we feel the danger and proceed in spite of these warnings that we are ripe for trouble. It is in these times that we become victim to the threat that we figuratively kick ourselves and say, "Well, you deserved that. You should have known better." The problem is that many of us go through this self-chastisement repeatedly and are resultantly no wiser.

There was once a very famous definition of insanity that declared it, "doing the same thing over and over again and expecting different results.[22] All of us should consider the choices we make in our lives. Are we making "risk assessments" when we consider whether to "stop" and check it out?

As parents, we make decisions for ourselves as well as our children, whether we know it or not. Just like the driver of our tourist van, he was responsible for us as well as himself. Knowing that the welfare of his passengers outweighed his own interest his decision was swift and concise, just say "no."

I recently spoke with a young woman considering beginning her adult life in the casual but intimate company of a young man. She did not consider the curious interest of her future children as they might ask her, "Why mom?" This is especially harder to do when you know in advance that you were warned against it and continued in spite of the warning voice.

---

[22] Albert Einstein

If we ask ourselves the honest question, we could say in most cases that we were in fact warned by someone. Warning could come in the form of a representative of faith, civil or public official or the "still small voice" within our own consciousness.

It is increasingly difficult to heed the warning voice when it is contrary to what we "want" instead of what we "need." This is where discipline and self-control plays a critical role and is the one thing in short supply in our society today. Discipline and self-control runs contrary to marketing ambitions to sell or consume product to generate increasing and immediate revenue.

Marketing ambition teaches that "if the demand for the product does not exist, then create it." Generate dissatisfaction in existing product so that a new one can improve your life because you deserve it. This directive plays into the attitude of entitlement which drives the addiction to debt and ultimate despair. It is a choice made with curiosity in the roadside bus which can overwhelm with trouble beyond imagination.

The lessons learned are to stay on task and be not distracted by those that could deter you from your appointed destination. These are Simple truths that serve the wise traveler along the road of life. They reach their destination in part by saying, "no thank you" to those along the way.

Truth, Basic #6:
> **Some things our children are taught
> fail the "common sense" rule.**

THE *"ILLOGICALITY"* OF EVOLUTION

(For the creation of life)

The process of evolution is widely accepted by academia of our day as an explanation of our existence. I do not doubt the logic of such an event; however, it being the secular version of our purpose and existence leaves countless holes in reason. The human body itself is a collection of elements normally found in the earth:

- Oxygen (65%)
- Carbon (18%)
- Hydrogen (10%)
- Nitrogen (3%)
- Calcium (1.5%)
- Phosphorus (1.0%)

- Potassium (0.35%)
- Sulfur (0.25%)
- Sodium (0.15%)
- Magnesium (0.05%)
- Copper, Zinc, Selenium, Molybdenum, Fluorine, Chlorine, Iodine, Manganese, Cobalt, Iron (0.70%)
- Lithium, Strontium, Aluminum, Silicon, Lead, Vanadium, Arsenic, Bromine (trace amounts)

These elements are common on the earth. It is the product that they came together to produce is what makes them uniquely special. All of these elements could be identified as inanimate, yet they are what we use to walk, run and play. Somewhere along the way, are we to believe that these combined materials evolved to create a consciousness, a state of being self-aware and capable of thought and reason? This is the widely accepted leap of logic that is accepted in the halls of modern science today. It would appear to me that this leap of logic illogical leap.

No matter what skillful manipulation of colorful language may be employed, the concept simply makes no sense. It would seem logical to me that these elements can collide together by whatever combination, permutation or imagination that could be infinitely imagined over infinite millennia and never produce consciousness, sense of self or presence of soul. Every cell in the human body is more complex than any mechanical device that has ever or ever will be constructed by man. Man, in all of his wisdom and technology, has never been able to manufacture a human cell from scratch much less put billions of them together in

54

functional form. If evolution is true as it is presented to us, I have a scenario I would like you to consider.

A wrist watch is something very common in our everyday lives. It is a relatively simple little device that keeps up with the passing seconds and hours of our lives as the earth progresses in its elliptical course around the sun. As we go to work and play, time is critical, we must keep up with it to fulfill our obligations.

The Swiss have been known to produce accurate time pieces for decades. They have the reputation of making watches that will keep very accurate time using care and precision. Each contains dozens of little pieces with notches or gears. The material is made of various types of metal commonly found in the ground. The ore is smelted to form metal. The metal is skillfully processed to the tolerances specified by the designer. The small pieces of metal are then skillfully shaped to form the individual pieces to form a working watch.

Each of these pieces is shaped to perfection and must be in harmony with each other. Their anticipated integration works in concert to rotate the independent hands of the watch to point at a specific number at a specific time and in a specific sequence. The tolerances must be exact. Any deviation from this will produce less than perfect results. Each of these individual pieces is a work of art in themselves.

Once the individual components are completed, they must be assembled by a master watch maker. This would be someone who understands the entire process, what each piece is and how they fit together. Great care would be taken to assure that each piece would be placed in the exact right place and in the exact right order.

After the internal components were completed an attractive housing would need to be constructed to protect the components from the harsh environment it would need to be in to operate. The main drive shaft would need to penetrate the housing on which two "hands" would mount. One of the hands is long and one is short. Each of these has its individual purpose. The hands may have a luminescent chemical on them so that you could tell the time after dark.

Of course, the face of the watch must be transparent so you can see where the hands are pointing. Now that the watch is completed with the internal components, the face, hands placed and the transparent cover, it is necessary to install a back to make the seal of the components complete. The back must be removed however, in the case that maintenance is needed. Therefore a long threaded cut is made in a matching back that will fit exactly in place to make a perfect fit. All of the components fit with exacting tolerances.

Wait, the completed watch needs to be convenient and comfortable to wear. Oh, and we need to be sure it is attractive too. After all, who wants to wear an ugly watch? Let's fashion a wrist band that will complement the watch and provide a functional means to attach it to the arm of the wearer. It needs a power source, something to make it come to life, something to make the combined pieces move in harmony. It needs to be flexible but strong so that it will stand up to the everyday hazards life may offer or alas, the job is not complete.

Just like each individual part of a Swiss watch, each of the organs in the human body is precious in and of itself; however, infinity more complicated. The watch has dozens of pieces that are fit together with precision and in concert with each other. Likewise, the human body has many different organs that fit together with precision and in concert with each other but with infinitely more complexity. With all of the various parts fitted perfectly together, the human body and the watch does have one thing in common; until the creator lovingly winds the spring, or adds life (soul), both will lay motionless.

Consider this possibility: Disassemble a fine Swiss watch, completely. Take every gear, every screw, every component of every kind (if you can) apart and hold them in the palm of your hand. Contemplate the beauty and complexity of each of them individually. Now, with the palm of your hand open, toss them into the air as far as you can...don't worry, using the theory of Evolution as taught by Darwin, they should all fall down into a working piece of mechanical art to tell perfect time. Well if not the first time, maybe the second. If that does not work just do it about a million times a million times over a millennia and it should work, right?

Why should you believe this? Because those who have the "schooling" to know these things as taught by those who are "experts" tell us that this is how it is and we should believe it.

Every item manufactured by man has base materials. These materials have chemicals and components that make the product. Every product given enough time and left to its own will corrode to its most stable form in the conditions it is left in. How much faster will the process proceed if it is dropped on the floor a million times a million times?

I believe...............that each of us has the ability to know what is truth and what is not through the *director* [23]given us by the "creator." We were built by a visionary, a master who had a plan and a design. Each part is precious in and of itself. It is assembled with precision and skill, placed in a protective housing and given hands to point and a mind to direct them.

The world is so full of "wisdom" that it has lost common sense. What is real and what is not is in itself up for questioning.

---

[23] Alma 37:38

Truth, Basic #7:
  Some things are not to be understood right away. It takes a while.

LIFE IS A PURSUIT
OF UNDERSTANDING

Though the evolutionary process falters under the scrutiny of common sense, it is very applicable as we consider how we learn and grow. Evolution is described as an "unfolding or coming out, our working out; process of development, as from a simple to a complex form, or of gradual progressive change"[24] which seems to me to describe life itself more than anything else I can think of.

For many years scientists of the world have debated the origin of life on earth and the development of the universe. Opposing views rage even today as those who

---

[24]Encarta Dictionary

profess to know such things and display the earthly accolades on the wall, say that it was formed by the natural occurrences of the cosmos? Those who embrace the doctrines of The Church of Jesus Christ of Latter day Saints declare that all that we know and see were subject to the Master's hand, the same as we know as Jesus of Nazareth.

In the Pearl of Great Price we read, *"God saw that they were good, and he stood in the midst of them, and he said: These I will make my rulers, for he stood among those that were spirits and he saw that they were good..."*[25] The progression for each of us began before we were born to mortality. As pre-mortal spirits we were in a position to distinguish ourselves as "good." Now the distinction beyond that may be up for debate. If there was good, could there have also been a bad, or perhaps not so good? We do know of one who was thrust out of Fathers presence for rebellion. And if there was good and at least rebellion, there must have been some that were better than just "ordinary good." Otherwise, why would the Lord have pulled out the "good" as the rulers? Surely "good" was a distinguishing characteristic in the spirit world.

Further we know there was a progression of understanding and obedience in the pre-mortal existence as stated,

> *"...we will go down for there is space there*
> *and we will take of these materials and we*
> *will make an earth whereon these may dwell.*
> *And we will prove them herewith to see if they*

---

[25] Abraham 3:23

will do all things whatsoever the Lord their
God shall command them."[26]

We had progressed as far as we could in that state of existence. Those that "kept their first estate" are all of those who heard the words of His voice. Following the Savior's plan, we earned a right to take our place among the sons and daughters of God to occupy these mortal bodies and dwell on the earth He made for us. Now as we progressed in this "evolution of understanding" we were sent with the charge described in the following scripture,

> *"And they who keep their first estate shall be*
> *added upon and they who keep not their first*
> *estate shall not have glory in the same kingdom*
> *with those who keep their first estate and they*
> *who keep their second estate shall have glory*
> *added upon their heads forever and ever."*[27]

The process of "understanding" is described as "the mental quality, comprehension, knowledge, discernment, awareness or to stand among."[28] How is it that we can come to an understanding of a subject without studying it or becoming subject to the practice? It is through the experience of study or practice that one can understand the subject of which we desire to know.

---

[26] Abraham 3:24-25
[27] (Abr3:26):
[28] Encarta Dictionary: (North American)

The implementation of the plan of salvation began when Adam and Eve were placed in the Garden of Eden. They were commanded not to partake but given the agency to choose. Understanding that there was no other way to gain knowledge, Eve partook, beginning our mortal journey.[29] This earth is the proving ground for each of us to do likewise. Because of our various circumstances in life, we are faced with countless challenges. Choices must be made every day, every hour, and even every moment of our lives. We choose our thoughts, our actions, our words and our deeds. Do they reflect an understanding of ourselves as temporary beings that evolved to a consciousness where to "eat drink and be merry, for tomorrow we die" is our main goal in life?

Certainly, this is the attitude of much of the world around us. However, some of the people of the earth believe they are subject to an almighty God of some form. This is a spiritual prompting of where they came from. However, their progress in the "evolution of understanding" has failed to find where the truth exists.

In returning to the definition of *understanding* we know that it includes "to stand with or among." To have a real understanding of the Lord and His ways is to receive the doctrine of Jesus Christ into our lives. Once this has occurred, we will stand with and be among those that the Lord declared as "good." To understand (with a perfect knowledge) and to turn away is to be classified among those few who are called the Sons of Perdition.

---

[29] Mos 3:17

I believe that most people, given the chance, would choose happiness and freedom. However, we know through sad experience that there are many who choose sadness, pain and suffering. It is this very knowledge that is in itself a testament of our evolution of understanding. It is the experience of life that provides the vehicle to make this happen. The Lord reveals His truth *"line upon line, precept upon precept, here a little, there a little."*[30]

A child is born into the world completely dependent upon its caregiver for every necessity of life. Here a little, there a little, he is taught, nurtured and helped to develop. He learns to walk, to talk and eventually reason for himself. His understanding of matters comes through the things he studies and becomes subject to through experience. *

Our understanding improves as our life progresses. Our decisions and the decisions of others have an effect on us. We develop wisdom which can only be acquired through life experiences and change us for the better or allow them to define our inability to change.

As I have come to know and understand these principles, I look back on my life and understand how the Lord works. It is truly line by line and precept by precept and our life's tapestry is a culmination of countless stitches placed in proportion to every experience we have had. It is on display for all to see who we are and what we have become. This vision adds to our level of understanding.

Life's various experiences are the building blocks to our personal evolution. What choices have we made in

---

[30] D&C 128:21

connection with the circumstances of life? The longer we live, the more experiences we have in a wider range of understanding. We are able to make better choices because we have seen the outcomes either in our lives or those around us. It is through the correct use of choices that we can obtain a level where our environment is a product of our collective choices. This is where we can rightfully use the word *wisdom.*

Wisdom is described in the following manner, "power of judging rightly and following the soundest course of action based on knowledge, experience and understanding." [31] President Gordon B. Hinckley's famous quote now has new meaning, "You can be wise and happy or stupid and miserable."[32]

There are several billion people on the earth now going through the same mortal process as we are. There are countless interactions between these souls which produce infinite possibilities and consequences. The Lord sent us here to gain experience, to understand the correlation between choice and consequence, to learn and to grow. Through the evolution that comes through the aging process of "one-day-at-a-time," we slowly become who we are today.

To know God is to begin with the spirit that dwells within saying in our mind, "There is more to this life than what I can see with my mortal eyes." Taking that thought to the point of study and with faith to prayer, is when the Lord

---

[31] Encarta Dictionary (North America)
[32] Gordon B. Hinkley March 1, 2007 Ensign

reveals His truth a little at a time. If we "keep our first estate" or move correctly with the new found knowledge, we are given more light and knowledge from Him. The correct application of this new knowledge begins the process over again until we have an understanding of the Restored Gospel that cannot be denied. For as Joseph said, "I knew it, and I knew that God knew it, and I could not deny it, neither dared I do it, at least I knew that by so doing I would offend God."[33]

Consider the following examples:

- I did not understand the spiritual and expansive happiness associated with a family sealed by the *covenant* until I created one.
- I thought I understood the meaning of Love until I had a loving wife, children and grandchildren who call me on the phone and utter among their first words "POPS."
- I thought I understood the meaning of Love until I stood on the hillside of the Mount of Olives and felt the love of the Savior as he willingly passed through the gates of Jerusalem to his crucifixion.
- My capacities for love, happiness and joy are only expanded by my capacities in understanding levels of pain, suffering and misery.
- My value of life became more cherished as I witnessed the senseless taking of it.

---

[33] JSH 1:25.

- I thought I understood the new and everlasting covenant until I received personal revelation concerning it on the top of Mount Phillips.[34]
- I thought I understood the joy of living until my life was nearly lost.
- I thought I appreciated the blessings of this Gospel until I saw the lives of those without it and the happiness they are missing.
- I thought I knew the pain of sin until I witnessed the agony of others as they suffered its consequences and the destruction of families.

Each day brings new experiences. With each experience we can add to our spiritual evolution. This evolution however is multi directional. We can choose to learn from our experiences and evolve positively or degenerate in a negative evolutionary process. The choice is ours. This too, is part of the divinely orchestrated plan.

The process of evolution describes our very lives. In the end, all that we take with us beyond the veil is our knowledge and experiences. How far will we have evolved by then? Life is an evolution of understanding.

---

34 Chapter 15: "The new and everlasting covenant"

SECTION 2

Advancing *truth*
As
Held by our youth

Now we advance a bit in knowledge and understanding.
As our children grow, they are taught many "facts." This
material is presented as facts because there is no allowance
for spirituality in the halls of academia. The challenge for
this emerging age group is to separate the facts from theory
or outright fiction.

THE LANDING ZONE

I have often wondered how the game of life is played. Specifically, what was it that determined where I would land in the fabric of life? Most would say that it is purely a random thing, that there is no rhyme or reason why I was born into one family and you into another. One child was born into poverty and one into royalty and wealth. The question, in this context is not so much why but what we should do once we land.

As a veteran, I understand somewhat what it means to face uncertain circumstances and to be trained to deal with them whatever they may be. Preceding the invasion of French soil in Normandy, paratroopers were dropped all over the countryside to address certain objectives. In many cases, the troops overshot the targets or were otherwise dropped into circumstances extremely contrary to what was planned. Once they jumped out the door, their destination was sealed. They were going to land where they were going to land and there was nothing they could do about it. They had to make the best of what they had before them. Their training, knowledge and capabilities lead them and they had to pursue their objective.

Some did not make it to the ground. They were shot while descending still strapped to their chutes. Others landed on roof or tree tops and were injured before they could touch the ground. Still others landed so far off target that they struggled to determine where they were and how they were going to get to their objective. Others still, were so injured by the jump that reaching and completing the objective was no longer an option or priority. Survival and extraction became their only option.

When considering the circumstances of life our placement in life is like a landing zone. Although, I am sure it was divinely orchestrated, our mortal understanding of it may be that we were dropped to the earth and we landed where we landed. Our circumstances are different. However, our ability to survive depends on our training, knowledge and understanding of who we are and what we can become. We credit it to luck (good or bad) and face it for what it is and move on.

Those today that complain about their disadvantage in the "lottery of life" are those that believe they were not dropped in the right place. They did not have a chance to succeed. That concept has some merit. However, there was probably another soldier that landed right beside him that managed to succeed and accomplish his goal.

The difference is that when he hit the ground he realized he was off target but with skill and application of his training, he kept his head down, stayed out of sight, applied persuasion when needed and returned to friendly territory with a story to tell.

Now, it would be a fair question to ask where this training came from if you entered the battlefield of life as a newborn. The spirit that occupies our body are eternal. We came from the creator and He gave us an opportunity to have an experience on earth and to learn the lessons that can only be gained here.

This spirit came with some "base programming" that many know as a conscience and is the feeling of right and wrong inherent in each of us. In many cases the wrong choices are made so often that the conscience becomes ineffective. It is the base for our ambition, drive and sense of self-preservation in doing good. This is what makes the difference between those who choose to give up and to blame others and those who rise above it and move on.

Those who land on target and reach the objective as planned, gather in the company compound and share short stories recalling the events over a cup of hot chocolate and a pastry. Others, dealing with the extreme difficulty of escape or evasion behind enemy lines will struggle to survive minute by minute, day by day. They will have to use all of the training they have plus the desire from within to reach their friends in the compound.

Their experience will be very different. It can be filled with stress, confusion and even the sense of betrayal as they feel left behind or forgotten or left in hostile territory to fend for themselves. In the end, the successful journey will grant them a seat beside their comrades at the table enjoying their company and the same hot chocolate and pastries that they had.

The two brothers sitting side by side will have had a very different experience in the battlefield of life as they share in the equal reward of safety and freedom. Some will have physical or emotional scars, or both. They will carry the memory of their past forever in their minds. Some will become bitter as they consider how they were mistreated. Some will write it off as bad luck. Others will blame those in charge with dereliction of duty as they had to suffer the consequences of their poor execution of the planned operation.

The best of them however, will consider it a blessing and feel lucky to be among those who were able to broaden their horizons and experience. When the time comes to "tell the tale" of the events of the day, those who were dropped off target and had the most difficult time in their survival will be those who gather the largest crowd as they explain how they accomplished their goals, how they overcame perilous conditions and advanced against insurmountable opposition.

It is truly a blessing to land in a friendly zone, a family who will nurture you in the light of the gospel, but it is equally a blessing to be dropped in a hostile zone where you have to make it out on your own. It can make you stronger. It makes you tougher and your memory of the struggle to reach your objective will forever give you the strength to face the continuing life's opposition and have no fear. You will have knowledge of facing the enemy and know all too well how to survive behind enemy lines.

This is how I have come to understand and accept my placing in the fabric of life. I would never want to live through the early years again but I would not trade them for any of those of my brothers more pleasant upbringing. I am what I am because of where I came from and what I had to do to get here. This is a blessing; I accept this and thank the Lord for dropping me in this hostile place and giving me direction of my objective that will supply peace, love and happiness.

Furthermore, I believe that if I had any influence on my earthly "LZ" (landing zone), I would have looked at the *challenges*, "just there" on the map labeled "the hot zone" and said, "That looks interesting sir, send me there."...and I suspect, you did the same.

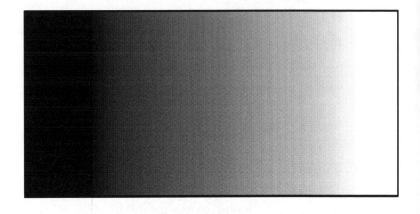

THE GRADIENT OF LIFE
(Where are you today?)

There is a gradual transition between total blackness and total white in any spectrum of color. The transition can be depicted in the selection process of a computer program in a scale called a Gradient. While assigning a color to a specific project, I was asked by the program to place the cursor on the above scale and "click to choose." As the mouse moved from one side to the other of the spectrum, the shade was displayed in the selection window. "How easy it is," I thought, "to change from total blackness to brilliant white by moving along the spectrum of possibilities."

Following the project, my mind wandered to consider the implications of that simple but effective gradient scale. It contained gradual but incremental differences between the two extremes. Every possible shade between black and white were represented. Within the realm of possibilities, all options were included. Could this gradient represent a selection process in what *shade* we choose to live our lives?

As I have come to know the youth of the Church through my years of responsibility and remembering my own kids, I know that many of them (if not most) live several different lives. They have one life for home, one for church, one for school and one for the "other" times. Their assignment on the gradient scale of conduct is often starkly different.

In one particular exercise, I asked a group of youth to place a mark on the scale to represent their level of conduct in each of these separate "lives." In most cases the distance between the lowest (darkest) behaviors and highest (lightest) behaviors represented half the total spectrum length. In other words, if total blackness was assigned a value of zero (0) and the lightest edge was assigned one hundred (100), there would be a full fifty (50) point spread.

Of concern here, is that these value assignments were made by our *very best,* our active youth who sit every Sunday listening to the lessons and telling leaders all the things they have been taught we want to hear. I have come to know by painful circumstance that our youth live in conflicting worlds and to survive, they believe that they must participate in the *game*. This "game" is often deadly and can lead to the loss of innocence, virtue or even their lives.

When assigning a Normal Distribution (bell curve) over the plotted median (average) conduct gradient plots from the youth, a value of seventy (70) points was identified. In the academic halls of our institutions of higher learning, this score is the lowest possible grade for one to receive a passing grade. Should we, as leaders, be concerned?

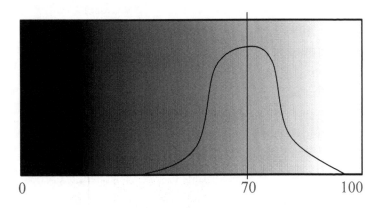

If this condition exists in our youth, how much more prominate is it in our own lives? Are we different at work than we are at home? Do we have one set of rules in the classrooms of the Church building and another on the golf course? The honest answer to this question would usually bring difficult self-reflection and cause for personal readjustment.

There are many cases where I have sat in counsel with a Sister who describes the conduct of her spouse that is very contrary to the behavior I would think him possible of. Brethren have described their wives behavior that makes me question my recollection of the person in question, "Surely, this cannot be her! I know her, and do not think she could do such a thing." In some cases, the accusations are exaggerated but in many unfortunate situations, the circumstances are factual. In these situations, I can only conclude that the conduct of the person "I know" is plotted on the gradient scale in a very different place than the one they reflect to others.

Often, people act the way they know we expect them to. When at school or at work, they exercise the level of conduct (gradient plot) that represents the environment. As they live in *different worlds*, they behave differently thereby causing extreme variations in their life's shade between black and white.

If we recognize the black as evil (carnally minded) and the white as good, (spiritually minded) we can begin to relate it to the struggle between the opposing forces for the souls of man. As we wake up every morning, we begin our day somewhere on the gradient scale. It may be a direct reflection of the conduct of the previous day or the beginning of a "new day," a day of reckoning or recompense. In any event we can plot our position on the scale representing our conduct between good and evil.

Where are we today? Where are we on the scale between evil and good, light and darkness? It would be good to consider that the variation between the plots should be minimal.

The Savior Jesus Christ was the only mortal in the history of mankind that lived a perfect life and the only one that can claim placement of perfect white. It is not possible for us to claim this position but we can claim the destination.

Hopefully, all of us seek to live in the light where we are free from the gradient grey of misconduct. In this area of white we find joy, happiness, love and charity. As we recognize that this level of conduct is where we want to stay, free from darkness, it is easier to perpetuate. However, there are many who feel that they can dwell in the light and wander to the "dark side" for a temporary relief from the restrictions of a disciplined life style. The perceived success of this activity is an effective act of deception orchestrated by the master of lies.

This image is graphically personal to me as I relate to an experience I had many years ago. While preparing to scuba dive in the Gulf of Mexico, I sat on the railing of the starboard stern preparing to fall back into the six foot seas. With the boat rising and falling in the heavy surf of the rough sea, I pushed off for a rearward water entry. As fate would have it, I pushed off at the peak of the wave leaving a considerable distance between my position on the boat and the declining surface of the ebbing sea swell. As I floated on the rising wave, I was violently introduced to the then plunging boat riding the wave downward. The bottom of the boat met my head offering no degree of mercy

to my obviously inferior object of density.

As the blood entered the water and the stars entered my eyes, I struggled to clear the ocean from my lungs and mask.

After a moment or two, I collected myself sufficiently to scrutinize my situation. "Wait, where is my spear gun?" I thought, "It was in my arms only a moment ago." Fearing the worse, I looked down…into the darkened abyss below.

The water was deep there, we knew that, but I was prepared to survey the 125' ocean floor to hunt for a few big fish to bring home for dinner. Gently following the laws of nature, the sea and physics, my cherished 48" triple band teak and stainless spear gun was heading to the open sea floor far below. I knew that in my frazzled condition I had to make a difficult choice. To engage in a rapid decent to retrieve the gun that was barely visible now would soon enter a deepening darkness and put my life at risk. It was dark there and represented all that was bad despite my anxious but now altered ambitions.

As I looked up, I could see the rays of light penetrating the surface. I knew, there was safety there, up toward the light. At that moment, I was in the *gradient* of life's choices. Below was darkness and danger. I was tempted to enter its ever increasing darkened gradient chasing something of value to me. But, as it became ever more embraced by the shadows of the abyss I silently watched my faithful hunting companion disappear forever. Accepting its fate, I gathered my senses and gradually ascended to the surface with a bruised head and ego.

At some point in our lives, we must all make a similar decision; at what point of gradient behavior are we willing to accept? We are told that *"the Lord cannot look upon sin with the least degree of allowance."*[35] Does this mean that anything left of the perfect white line is unacceptable to him?

We are all given the same set of rules and guidelines. Some hear the message and some do not. In His infinite judgment and wisdom, justice will be served to all of us according to His perfect will. Our level of obedience to these rules is what we will be held accountable to. As we are given the greater light, we will be held to a greater standard.[36]

As we consider the perspective on the gradient image, we can take the discussion a bit further. It is customary that the transition from "light" to "darkness" is gradual in life's decisions also. One small move toward the darkness is followed by another allowing time to acclimate to the changing climate. It is also easier (and closer in proximity) to reach deeper toward the abyss. As the light

---

[35] Alma 45: 16
[36] D&C 82:3

fades into the darker phase of life, it is harder to ascend toward the light.

The powers of darkness have many allies that are determined to keep you where you are and have countless methods at their disposal including friends, peers, family, threats and intimidation. Before long, the dark regions of the gradient become *home* where light cannot penetrate. In my discussions with the youth, I asked them to designate a "zone" within the gradient to classify the boundaries between what is considered "cool" at school and church.

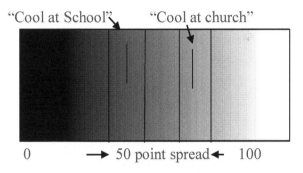

The insight was interesting. When I first identified the spread between the behaviors assigned by the youth, there was nearly a 50 point spread between their best and worst behavior. The center of these zones also represented the same spread on the gradient spectrum. The obvious conclusion is simple, in their attempts to be cool at school and cool at church, their behavior varies greatly.

The same exercise was then given to the adult youth leaders. Although their behaviors differed between work, home and church, the spread was much less severe. A tighter assignment of the dots on the gradient depicted a group of people who were very similar in all situations.

Youth are in the process of life's journey where they determine who they are and what they want to become. As a result, their behaviors vary as they experiment with different life styles, friends and behaviors. They travel through the gradient of life where the temperature of the water varies between the surface (warm) and the bottom (cold). They feel the variations of the thermals that travel along the way and decide where they are comfortable. They hear the voices of those calling out to them from the various locations within the gradient and ultimately make a decision where their life's placement should be.

Some choose an area of dimmed light and increased pressure near the center while others prefer the bottom where there is no place to go but up. Still, others prefer the light and warmth of the surface where freedom from the pressures and darkness of the deep are only a step away.

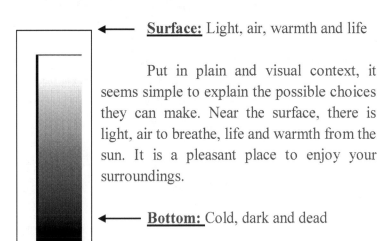

Surface: Light, air, warmth and life

Put in plain and visual context, it seems simple to explain the possible choices they can make. Near the surface, there is light, air to breathe, life and warmth from the sun. It is a pleasant place to enjoy your surroundings.

Bottom: Cold, dark and dead

In contrast, the bottom represents all that is unpleasant. Because there is no air to sustain human life, there is also eventual death. The greater depths produce greater pressures. Because of the distance from the source of the light and heat from the sun, it is very dark.

Through the accumulation of life's experiences, the adults who have survived the journey through the gradient have come to understand for themselves where life is most comfortable. They have witnessed the cold and darkness of sin and choose to avoid it at all cost. They have responsibilities for children that depend on them to protect them from the dangers lurking in deep and dark waters but as children often do, when given a chance, they will head straight for the object provoking curiosity as they hear the voices of intrigue and excitement.

There, outside the walls of the protected cocoon, they can experience the excitement of danger and feel the rush of adrenaline supplying their system with a "change" from the ordinary humdrum of life not knowing that there is no support in the water that will draw them to a certain abyss of darkness and misery.

In all that we do and say, it is our responsibility as adult youth leaders to convince them that that lurking in deep waters is hazardous to their health. There is no simple method for this goal other than to love them, become a part of their lives and teach them the doctrine of life and the joy associated with the breath of life in the warmth of Gospel air. It is cool to live and have the freedom to play on the surface. It is not cool to be trapped in the abyss of the darkness of the deep. Through prayer and fasting we can make a difference in their lives; we just need to stay on task and never give up!

We should all examine our lives and determine our placement on the gradient scale of life and always ask ourselves the question, "Where am I today?

Truth, Advancing #10:
   Our youth need to learn the art of self-defense.

ARMOR OF GOD

There are many platitudes used in teaching the youth of the church. None is overused more than the phrase, *Armor of God!* I am reminded of a cartoon that depicts two oversized polar bears sitting down for their evening meal with an igloo in each hand. One turned to the other and said, "I love these things, crunchy on the outside, chewy on the inside."

Embedded in the levity there is an unintended message. We may have to have a hardened shell on the outside for protection from the enemy but we need to remain pliable on the inside to support life, tender enough to feel the spirit.

Armor is a protective shell worn to safeguard the body from objects intended to harm it. This is essential when you enter a situation where you are unable to know when and where you may become a target of the enemy. It is easy to stay out of harm's way when you know what direction it will be coming from and when. The problem is that in many cases, this is not possible. The mission of the soldier is to enter dangerous situations and to make them safe for others. Similar situations occur in the jobs of law enforcement and other professions.

We teach our youth to avoid potentially harmful situations. "Just say no" or "Just don't go" seems logical advice but assumes that we have the freedom to avoid any potential threat. However, the basic rule of warfare historically, is to defeat the enemy with overwhelming force (when you have no choice but to fight) sufficient to collapse their defenses. This can be done through sheer numbers in forces, firepower or technology. Sometimes our understanding of what this means may greatly disappoint us.

I have a good friend, a fellow soldier, who served in the conflict in Viet Nam. He was a decorated soldier serving as an operative in the Army's Special Operations. He relayed an experience to me of an occasion when he and his team had identified an entire valley that hosted a battalion size contingent of Viet Cong enemy soldiers.

As he and his team took cover, the B-52 bombers were called in to *clear* the threat from the area. Being highly effective in their task, the air was soon filled with the whistling sound of hundreds of bombs falling in succession to the earth below. The 500 lb. bombs impacted with the reverberation of an automatic rifle fire as the entire valley below filled with flames and debris. The leading edges of the shock waves from the concussion shattered all that stood in its path and compressed the blood to the innards of the body as a multi g-force impact struck them over a mile away.

Allowing time for the circulation to regain access to their exposed extremities, the team stood from their observation post to access the damage below. As the moment's passed, the rising plumes of smoke, blackened from burning debris and the smell of human suffering, he simply said, "it was gone; the valley disappeared." Nothing of what they were observing at that moment resembled anything similar to what they had seen only moments before. The entire shape of the landscape had changed. There were no trees, no canopy and no jungle. It was a smoldering landscape of fire, ashes and ruins. The mission was successful, or so it appeared.

Within moments, he recalls, there was small arms fire coming from the valley in their general direction. My friend could see the muzzle flashes from rifles "down there" being discharged as if to send a message to the greatest power on earth, that they lived; they survived and defiantly reentered the battle to fight another day.

Attrition is an effective tool of the enemy in our lives. He never gives up; he will never go away and will never admit defeat during the days of our mortal probation.

We will always be at war with this great enemy. It is his mission along with all of those that follow him to make us miserable like unto himself. We need all of the protection we can get; the best of which is to stay out of that dangerous valley where the enemy forces lurk.

The enemy will survive carpet bombing, sneak attacks and intimidation because they are many. Their goal is to convince us that there are more of them that there are of you (overwhelming force) so you might as well surrender. Though this is a wicked illusion, we know as the veil is lifted it is quite the contrary.

> *"And when the servant of the man of God was risen early, and gone forth, behold, an host compassed the city both with horses and chariots. And his servant said unto him, Alas, my master! How shall we do? And he answered, Fear not: for they that be with us are more than they that be with them."[37]*

The enemy has become skilled in the art of war in knowing our weaknesses and sending opposition our way in just the right caliber (drugs, alcohol, promiscuity) to intersect our position at just the right time (school, work, parties, friends, etc.). They will defiantly fire at us after we have called in the *big guns* to eliminate the threat ever reminding us that their opposition remains; and so it shall be. As cruel this may seem, it is actually a great blessing. As we come to know and understand the enemy and his tactics we can learn where and when they will strike us. As

---

[37] 2 Kings 6: 15, 16

a result, we will be prepared to overcome their opposition and push them back into their own lands.[38]

The problem with this type of enemy is that he plays for keeps. His purpose is not to only take your life but to steal your soul. This enemy is one to fear greater than the combined mortal armies ever assembled. *"And fear not them which kill the body, but are not able to kill the soul: but rather fear him which is able to destroy both soul and body in hell."*[39]

In all of the armor of man, none is designed to defend against such an enemy. The high speed projectiles being fired at us are not physical, they are spiritual. No amount of Kevlar (modern body armor) will prevent this mortal penetration.

Some years ago, I rushed to the bedside of my son in the intensive care unit of a distant hospital after being involved as a passenger in a fatal car accident. Though he suffered several broken bones that would linger for a lifetime, his life was preserved. Pleased to find him alert, he fondly welcomed my arrival and began to outline the details of the tragic incident. Seeing the marks on his chest, I asked of their origin. As he pulled away the hospital gown, I could see the outline of a long line going from over his shoulder toward his waist.

The contrast was distinctive as the broken blood vessels left the unique red hew against the white skin.

---

[38] Alma 43:44
[39] Matt 10:28

Recognizing it immediately, I withheld my response as he said, "Dad that was the seatbelt. It saved my life."

While on a weekend trip to Yellowstone National Park, he and some friends were traveling back to school when he heard a small voice, "put on your seatbelt." Moments after he complied with the prompting, it happened. As oncoming vehicle had lost control on the black ice covering the roadway. It struck them head on killing a small child sitting in the rear seat of the small family van.

My son survived with a broken back and multiple contusions. The instrument that saved his life was a small thing; it was only a seatbelt, but that small thing (the still small voice) spared his life as the B-52 were flying overhead deploying tons of deadly munitions in his path.

In this case the presence and the prompting of the Holy Ghost provided my son with a *spiritual Kevlar* that can be breached by no enemy. My son recited a promise in his patriarchal blessing that promised him safety if he remained faithful. "I knew that I would be okay Dad," he said, "because of my blessing."

What more can we teach our kids than to put on the Armor of God. More than anything else, we should teach them how to recognize the promptings of the Holy Ghost and to follow its directions. A hard shell can be a good thing as long as our spirits remain tender and malleable.

He will tell you when you are being shot at and where. He will tell you what valley to enter and when to stay away. He will also tell you what friends are the good ones and who are not so good and when necessary, if this be the Lord's will. Danger may be seconds ahead.

Not listening may be a fatal decision through loss of blessings, innocence or even their lives. There is always a good reason for the Holy Ghost to speak to us; after all, He is a member of the Godhead.

The spiritual Kevlar of the Holy Ghost cannot be penetrated. It is the perfect shield against any and all enemies. It can be worn by those who understand that they are a child of God, that He loves them and wants them to return to Him safely for the joys of eternity. War is too dangerous to walk around in unprotected; let's put on *the Armor of God*.

Truth, Advancing #11:
Youth are very susceptible to feelings of abandonment.

YOU ARE NEVER ALONE

It is as if the walls are converging to crush me, yet I see a perilous wave on its way to take me from my now comfortable perch. The elements of my emotional environment are conspiring to threaten my medicated peace. I struggle for sanity and seek comfort in my existence and a meaning for my status in life. Surely, I am not the first to ask these questions, am I? *"Where is the Lord... where art thou? And where is the pavilion that covereth thy hiding place?"[40]* In an infinitely inferior circumstance, I find myself asking that question many times as did my Brother Joseph Smith.

---

[40] D&C 121:1

There is just no telling what caused this condition. Maybe it was the crowds that were bumping and pushing as I tried to navigate in the mass of humanity in the amusement park whose purpose is to entertain and divert its guests from the cares of the world. In my mind however, there are too many to watch. I cannot access the potential threats lurking behind the deceptively friendly faces.

There appears to be no easy escape or protection of the hyper-vigilance tendencies that drive me to keep a safe and secure perimeter in this place. The only plausible solution is to surrender to the environment that encompasses me. Yet, I follow the one I love to her "happy place" and enjoy seeing the light in her eyes as she enjoys the good natured life's diversion under the black hat with two round *mouse* ears. She loves to smile and laugh and to be happy; a trait I long for.

In the following hours and days, the realities of the events sink into my psyche as I fight the emerging darkness. In a quiet place alone with my wife, I simply say, "sweetheart, I feel the walls coming in. I see the wave coming, the walls converging and I cannot stop them!" It was at this very moment that my phone rang delivering the voice of a *brother in arms*, one of only few that truly understand the human condition which plagues those who have witnessed the sights and sounds of suffering and conflict.

Many times in the past, we have shared each other's burdens regarding the issues associated with this condition. We do not ask others to understand nor can they give comfort or solace, only the voice of another *brother* can bring the reinforcements we need against this unforeseen and insurmountable enemy.

No one knew of my painful pending experience. I spoke of it to my wife only moments before though it had been building for days. I had tried to fight it off but failed and was at that moment facing a figurative incursion of an overwhelming force into my inner circle of protection, my inner circle of emotional control. No one knew, except me, my wife…and the Lord.

It was at His prompting that one of the only people who could provide help called me, just to say *Hello*. It was at that moment that I realized as I had a million times before, that the Lord is cognizant of me. He knew, and in His tender mercies spared me from this event that has overpowered me countless times before.

His pavilion is covered only by our mortality and the *one way* mirror that separates the earth from the watchful window of the creator, God Himself. Jesus Christ is more involved in our everyday lives that we may want to admit. He watches our every move and is aware of our trials and challenges. He is there to help, comfort and counsel when it is needed. He is however, true to the plan as counseled in the beginning to place us here on earth to learn from the environment crammed with opposition. At times it may seem to be unbearable. At times we are left to overcome them with a whisper of the spirit for support and at other times we feel alone. Though the enemy of all righteousness may want us to believe differently, our Heavenly Father is never far away.

Though, at the time I felt differently, I know now that my Father in heaven was not hiding in His pavilion, nor was he distant; He was sitting next to me saying, "Don't worry soldier, I've got your back!"

Though the crowds may push and pull, there will always be He who will never be off patrol. He will never be off duty or on leave. He will never be asleep or distracted. You will never be in a place where He cannot see or cannot hear. Not only do you not need to inform him of your condition, this "backup" knows your heart, your mind and your spirit. There is no better companion on this earth or the one to come. Remember, no matter where you are or where you go, He is always watching.

Truth, Advancing #12:
> **Youth are commonly fooled**
> **by the deceptions of man.**

WILDERNESS,
IS A STATE OF MIND

"Unimproved," is the term used by Realtors to define a piece of property that is found as nature has left it. In this context it is regarded as raw and implied to be of less worth than those who have had the hand of man place upon it. These large unimproved and uncultivated tracts represent an expanse of territory often described as wilderness. Wilderness is be defined in several ways. Here are a few:

- A mostly uninhabited area of land in its natural uncultivated state, sometimes deliberately preserved like this, e.g. a forest or mountainous region.
- An area that is empty or barren
- A piece of land that is deliberately not cultivated but is left to grow wild, e.g. in a garden

- A place, situation, or multitude of people or things that makes somebody feel confused, overwhelmed, or desolate
- A voice in the wilderness; to be giving advice or suggestions that are very unlikely to be followed.

Speaking of ourselves, wilderness represents the *natural state,* how it was before we were *cultivated* or *improved.* It is interesting, that these two words have relative meaning; what does it mean to be cultivated or improved? Depending on your perspective, ambitions or interest, they may have totally opposite meanings. To improve by one perspective would be destructive to another. Therefore, to be cultivated or improved is to be defined only by the subject of such action itself. If there were to be one definitive answer to this question it may be that it lies in the eyes of the creator.

Our Father in Heaven created this earth for us to *take care of, to till and cultivate.* By definition, wilderness or the earth in its earliest state is an *area that is empty or barren.* He also created our bodies and placed us here in this wilderness.

Predators thrive in the wilderness; it is their *natural* environment. They do not need clothing or shelter as we do. They have all they need to survive. With the hunting instinct and intellect they can feed themselves by shedding the blood of others to sustain their appetite. The wilderness is their world.

Maybe these improvements are not what the creator had in mind. "For the natural man is an enemy to God, and has been from the fall of Adam, and will be forever and ever unless he yields to the enticing of the Holy Spirit and putteth off the natural man."41 It is in this context that we begin to understand what genuine improvements may represent.

In this scripture it is implied that the Holy Spirit is the only thing which stands between him and the natural man. Without the Holy Ghost and his enticing's, man placed in the wilderness will remain there spirituality uninhabited, empty and barren to God's presence. This is where predators reside eager to shed the blood of their victims and to destroy the souls of man.

It is in this reasoning that we can begin to understand what the true meaning of improvement and cultivation really is. If we hold to the concept that it relates to overcoming the wilderness of the world, improvements are related to our ability to understand the word of God and improving our lives to follow Him. This can only be done by heeding to the promptings of the Holy Ghost. The cultivation of our testimony will be the nourishment that will sustain our spiritual lives to give us a glimpse into the eternities that lye above and beyond the barrenness of the wilderness of life.

It is also interesting to know that even in the most desolate and barren places on earth in the apparent absents of life that we learn that improvements and cultivation of

---

41 Mosiah 3:19

life reside in our own hearts in abundance as we seek and receive the enticing of the Holy Spirit. It is in these natural and remote places beyond the reaches of the deceptive improvements of the world that we find God.

Christ made the distinction speaking of King Solomon, *"Consider the lilies how they grow: they toil not, they spin not: and yet I say unto you, that Solomon in all his glory was not arrayed like one of these."*[42]

It was late one summer that we traveled to Italy to take in the sights of that beautiful nation. The city of Venice is beautiful by every description. At every turn, there is a picture perfect image to be captured for a lifetime of memories. A large cathedral is among the most beautiful and popular attractions there for this very reason.

Adorned with every imaginable quality of workmanship and ornate material, it demands respect for the countless hours of effort and imagination associated with its conception. It is a testament of man's capability for *improving* and *cultivating* the elements of the earth to create something magnificent to behold. Gilded mosaics cover the walls and ceilings of the edifice boasting over 8000 square meters. Surely, as the casual visitor enters its tall stone lined doors; they witness *improvements and cultivation* to the extent of mortal capability, considering that it was built in 832AD.

I am often puzzled at the long lines of those anxious to enter these places. As they look up, around and down they will see the sacrifice of the incalculable laborers

---

[42] Luke 12:27

associated with setting every stone in its proper place. Reaching for heaven, the spires pierced the altitudes of space to praise their God. It is ornate to say the least.

However, as I approached the scene, I witnessed the obvious skillful cultivation of the earth but felt empty when seeking escape from the wilderness of truth in the world. The spirit, (as I knew it) was not present in this place where many come for knowledge but yet captivated by its topical appeal.

It is by the enticing of the Holy Ghost that we are rescued from the wilderness. By definition, it is the only way. Does an earthly edifice of stone and plaster represent escape from spiritual wilderness or only a palace within its boundaries?

Many of us build these *escapes* from wilderness at home and even Church, when they are actually only simply shelters. Unless we heed to the enticing of the Holy Ghost, our souls cannot be cultivated and improved to advance beyond the condition of the desolate wilderness.

As Adam and Eve were thrown from the Garden of Eden into the lone and dreary world (wilderness) they had to start from *scratch*. Being cut off from the presence of the Lord they were separated from Him and His teachings and influence. Being in a state of sin, they were no longer allowed in His presence for He cannot be in the company of any unclean thing.[43] This is wilderness, barren and empty!

---

[43] 1 Nephi 15:34

To improve on our circumstance of the lone and dreary world we must seek improvements. We can build shelters that keep the rain off our heads and stop there, many do. As the amount of effort increases with each degree of improvement, our spiritual ambition is defined by our progress in this matter.

In the end the ultimate fact remains that the only improvement or cultivation that will be of any significant or meaningful measure will be delivered by the Holy Spirit. The Holy Ghost is the conduit to God, His truth, His influence and His message. It is the only respite from the wilderness of the world, its hollow teachings and ornate shelters.

As the daisy of the field is greater than the adornment of Solomon in all of his glory, our individual homes can be the residence of God himself as His spirit influence and message is represented by and through the spirit of the Holy Ghost. We do not need 8000 square meters of stone and marble. We do not need spires that touch the skies or tapestries or gilded mosaics. The world (wilderness) displays these for the praise of man, "look at me," it demands. "Look how special I am," they profess.

It is however, the tapestry and mosaics painted on the inner walls of our hearts and minds that can only be seen by God Himself that converts the wilderness of the world into the Garden of Eden and heaven on earth. It is the cathedral in our hearts that have us praise God in our actions thoughts and deeds and show who and what we are.

The Holy Ghost is the cool liquid stream of life in the desert, the shelter in the barren wilderness and sweet sustenance that nurtures a life of joy and happiness in the wilderness of pain and suffering. Although we were placed in the wilderness at birth, it is our choice how long we reside there. Sadly, most choose to build a shanty on the beach to avoid the effort of escaping the sea of unbelief and ignorance we know as wilderness.

Others however, recognize the divine and eternal spirit within them seeking further light and knowledge available in more fertile soil so they begin to travel. The Spirit will show them the way according to their desire, the Lords will and their worthiness. The scenes of wild and uncultivated entanglements will yield to pleasant meadows and eventually the promise land where we can be nurtured by the good word of God.

Once this personal understanding of self and eternal worth is established, there is no place on earth where *wilderness* is reality. It is just a place where no improvements or cultivation of man exists. Our hearts are walking palaces to our Heavenly Father where we see beauty and peace at every turn. When we achieve this condition, we will never again recognize wilderness, only the beauty and creations of God.

Truth, Advancing #13:
Youth are often
susceptible to depression.

LIVING WITHIN THE DARKNESS

It is a subject that no one wants to talk about. Our perception is that it is a reflection of the quality of our character or strength of spirit. It is often looked upon by many as a "defect," that somehow we are flawed. As a result, this false perception is effectively used by Satan to convince us of its reality. If we are flawed and defective, we are substandard and therefore are a burden to our families and society at large.

Depression and anxiety are common conditions to many of us. We live with it every day and battle its debilitating effects. Some days are better than others but its presence never withdraws its tentacles. To deny its effects is to turn away from an approaching tsunami and the devastation it will leave in its path. To many who take this path, divorce, sin and church discipline follow.

When we were first called as a Stake Presidency we knew the typical stint was 10 years. As we approached the 9th year I felt that my time was running short. In a Stake Priesthood Meeting I spoke of something there was little time left for me to tell. I wanted to reach deep within myself and give of my heart, something that I hoped would benefit my fellow man. I spoke of the "dark places" we must enter and only by faith would we emerge successfully. Life is filled with dark places that have no apparent light at the end of the journey. We are not sure where they will lead or what challenges we will face along the way, only that we need to go.

Following that meeting, the dive into the darkness of my memories past, put me on a path where only weeks of inner struggle could calm. I feel now as I did then, and countless times before, that this kind of life is unsustainable. Yet the days turn into years and look back with the darkened glass of reflection and only see the memories in shades of black and grey. Why would the Lord call such a person as this to various positions of responsibility in His church? I have asked myself this question many times.

I was interviewing a prominent sister in our stake for a temple recommend who shared these personal challenges. She had a loving and supportive husband and family. She was loved by all who knew her. She lived in a handsome home and her husband was well respected in the community and was a good provider. They were blessed with wonderful children who followed them in the faith.

There was no logical basis for this condition but it existed all the same.

It was at that moment that I realized of the three members of the Presidency that could have interviewed her that day, it was me. It was no coincidence. I was able to relate to her in a very special and personal way and was uniquely equipped to do. The Lord knew what she needed and put us together. Although neither was healed that day, the candid exchange of feelings and ideas was a blessing to us both. The reality of a cure is problematic. Though there are many drugs that claim a cure, their greatest benefit is to "mask" the pain.

Depression has been described by the medical profession as a disease. Researchers have noted differences in the brains of those who are depressed from those who are not. The part of the brain that stores memories, the hippocampus, is smaller with fewer serotonin receptors for those who suffer. Serotonin is the chemical that allows communication between nerves in the brain and the body. Though researchers do not know why the hippocampus is smaller for some, they do believe that when the stress hormone Cortisol is produced in excess, it becomes toxic or poisonous to the hippocampus. When this condition exists in a person there are many events that can trigger the damaging mental condition:

- Abuse
- Certain Medications
- Conflict
- Death or a loss

- Genetics
- Major events
- Personal problems
- Serious illness
- Substance Abuse

I am certain that there were happy times that occurred in the first 18 years of my life; I just cannot remember one. I do however have countless memories of the bad times. It would appear that not only do I have a smaller hippocampus; it is filled with only the bad memories. Although this is not what I want, it seems to be out of my control.

My "happy times" as a child were when I was alone in the woods away from the stress and conflict ever present in my home. It was not until I was a married young adult with children that I was forced to deal with my problem. Knowing that my path was leading to disaster, the Lord placed a good soul in my path to help me through.

One of the things I have noticed is that in most cases, only a soldier can comfort a soldier. Only a mother can comfort a mother and people who are outside the level of understanding of this disease are often clueless on how to help. It simply does not make sense to them! They may say, "Why are you sad? I don't understand!"

I have a loving and supportive wife. She would do anything to help me in any way. There could not be found a sweeter spirit than she to provide love and support. However, when it comes to depression or anxiety she does not understand. She is a happy, loving soul who sees the good in everyone and enjoys laughing and spending time with friends. I stick to myself and would just as soon be alone than in the company of anyone except my closest friends.

I have some experience on how the church is organized. It is wonderful. Within this organization are counselors, leaders and teachers. Before every major calling such as Bishops, Stake Presidencies, Mission Presidents, and Auxiliary presidencies, we have some orientation before the person serves. If this procedure is followed on earth in the imperfect mortal reality, should we not suppose that it took place in the pre-mortal, perfect world?

I believe that it would be safe to suppose that before we came to fulfill the most important element of our eternal existence, we would have had a chat with someone, perhaps the Savior Himself. Further, that He being perfect in His knowledge and understanding would have known what life circumstances we would face and what challenges were going to be placed in our earthly *back pack*. In addition, I am sure that He told me that this emotional challenge was going to be a part of my life but one I could overcome and "give me experience and be for my good."[44]

Though I know this to be true for me, the "back pack" has become very burdensome at times. Yet, all of those who carry it should do so for the welfare of others. Inside that bag are many experiences that can be of benefit

---

[44] D&C 122:7

to others. On many occasions, when the "trigger" was being pulled on my emotional stability, I would receive a call from someone I loved and respected who helped. Likewise, I have been used many times in the hands of the Lord to provide comfort for those of similar condition.

In the Stake where I served, sixty percent of the households were single and seventy five percent were without Melchizedek Priesthood. Looking at these numbers, there is plenty of reason to entertain anxiety as we understand what needs to be done to bring the full blessings of the Gospel in these homes. For the most part however, the families were not depressed, they were excited. They rejoiced in their ability to serve in whatever way they could. They had sufficient for their needs and were happy serving the Lord.

To all of those who say to people like me, "You have no reason to be unhappy," I agree. I take comfort in the fact that I know that the Lord knows who I am and what challenges I am facing. I take comfort in the fact that whatever challenges I have; they pale in comparison to my brother or sister who may be sitting next to me. I take strength from those who endure their trials better than I and see the goodness and joy in the world. I enjoy serving in the Kingdom and surrounding myself with things I know come from God. I enjoy looking into the faces of the innocent children with the light of life and hope in their eyes. I enjoy witnessing the superb decision making capabilities of an average tree squirrel caught off guard. I enjoy seeing life in the little things that are going about the fulfillment of their appointment to enjoy the *measure of their creation.*

The human brain is an interesting instrument. It is nearly endless in its capabilities and complexities. Each of us are blessed with one unique to ourselves. The Lord gave it to us to fulfill His purposes as we discover our own.

Some of us live within the darkness from choice or consequence. No matter what condition we live in, the Lord had given us His light. We can choose to follow this light from the darkness or ignore and accept our depressed condition as an irreconcilable fact. It is important for us to remember that, *"men are that they might have joy."*[45] Realizing first hand that this statement is easier to say than apply, Christ is the answer to all.

It was through my personal relationship with Him that I found comfort. It was, and is, through my understanding of His unquenchable love for me that I felt strength and comfort. I know that my small hippocampus gives me larger understanding which may give me the advantage in some ways. For this, I am thankful.

---

[45] 2 Nephi 2:25

Truth, Advancing #14:
For the first time in their lives,
youth must overcome barriers on their own.

BREAKING BARRIERS

In primary, we are taught about the time we lived with our Heavenly Father in the pre-existence. As spirit children of the Eternal God, we had progressed as far as we could in spiritual form and could go no farther without gaining an earthly body and experiencing mortality. A barrier was before us that must have seemed insurmountable. We knew that no unclean thing could dwell with God but that a body was necessary to progress. However, with that body came mortality, agency and sin which would bring about a separation from the God and the eternal home that we loved. How could we overcome this barrier?

A great council was therefore called where all the sons and daughters of God agreed to follow His plan of salvation. Our eldest brother Jesus Christ would atone for our sins and provide a path back to Heavenly Father[46]. The barrier was broken, the plan was put in place and we joyfully continued, anxious to face the challenges that life would bring.

However, life has brought us many challenges. Man has overcome the physical challenges of physical mobility by learning to walk and the challenge of communicating by learning to speak and the challenge of choice by learning to reason. With each of these accomplishments came a successful breach of the barrier. The strength necessary to overcome these barriers gave us growth, experience and wisdom. As a result, we learned what barriers looked like and how to overcome them, so long as they were familiar.

Sometimes, it would appear that with the successful breach of each obstacle another one stronger, wider and taller would always present itself just beyond it. After a while, we can become weary of the continual need for exertion and just surrender in the shadow of yet another barrier and say, "It is just insurmountable."

I once accompanied a group of Boy Scouts to the Philmont reservation in Cimarron, New Mexico. After days of grueling hikes and facing yet another steep incline, two boys plopped down beside the trail and declared that they were not going to go any farther. Of course, it was an absurd statement, as they had no choice but to go forward. The obstacle just seemed insurmountable, and given the option, they were ready to give up. After a time of *gentle*

---

[46] Mos 4:1-3

persuasion, they picked themselves up, wiped of their faces and moved up the trail.

Surely, there are many times we are ready to give up. We have had enough and our internal pressure gauges release the steam of frustration and anxiety which prompt us to stop in our tracks and to rest where we are. In fact there are many who do exactly that, but it is most unproductive and leads to physical and spiritual atrophy.

Mediocrity lives in the place between the walls of two barriers in our lives, the one behind and the one forward, standing in our path. Because of the obstacles daunting appearance, we may choose not to challenge it. It will take too much work and we convince ourselves that we are happy where we are. We have achievements that are sufficient, we have gone far enough. We convince ourselves that we have learned enough and need no more. Pride and haughtiness often accompanies this state of mind.

People that remain in this state will be met by those who pass us by on the trail of life toward a higher destination. Others will politely leave us in our tracks and scale the barrier impeding our advance. They often meet with ridicule from those leaning from the windows of the great and spacious building on the precipice of the chasm that separates them from the tree of life. We are all capable of so much more than we can imagine. Often it is not until we are challenged in something we cared about until we reach deep inside to pull out more than we think we have.

In my tenure as a youth leader over the years, many of the youth activities were carefully designed to push them beyond their comfort level, to help them see what they are capable of and what they can accomplish. It does not matter where this lesson is learned because once it is, it is a new standard that will benefit them in all walks of life for the rest of their lives. It makes them better at everything they do as a person, a missionary, a student, a husband, a wife, a father, a mother and a child of God. Once we learn that we have no barriers that we cannot overcome, we can accomplish many great and important things.

Heavenly Father has given us families to help us along this obstacle course of life. In most cases the family helps us through these challenges and encourages us to stretch beyond our comfort level, understanding that growth lies beyond. However, many families leave much room for improvement as they facilitate a sedimentary and/or restrictive environment discouraging new challenges.

If you have ever met or worked with someone who is not afraid of new barriers, you are a lucky person. They are filled with enthusiasm for their work and the challenges ahead. There is nothing that they cannot do because they know what it means to face insurmountable challenges, what is necessary to overcome them and the great joy that lies beyond. They work hard; they never stop and they rely on the Lord because they know all things are possible unto Him.

> *"I will go and do the things which the Lord*
> *hath commanded for I know that the Lord giveth*
> *no commandments unto the children of men save*

He shall prepare a way for them that they may
accomplish the thing which he commandeth
them. "[47]

Nephi was an example to all of us in how to rely on
the Lord to overcome barriers. Many barriers truly are
insurmountable! We cannot overcome them without our
Heavenly Father. The people that understand this principle
fill Priesthood, Relief Society, Sunday School, Primary
classrooms and homes in the kingdom of God as it sprawls
across this planet. They will no more be turned from their
seemingly impossible journey through endless
insurmountable barriers than attempt to reverse the flow of
the mighty Missouri river with an outstretched hand.

They will go *Forward in Faith*[48] not knowing that
the world tells them that it cannot be done. The mothers
will continue to build the lives of their precious children
driving them to greater and greater heights not fearing the
size or strength of opposition. As the sons of Helaman did
in earlier days, they will march in formation, weapons in
hand listening to the cadence of the heart beating within
their chest testifying that Jesus is the Christ, and in His
service rivers flow up hill, mountains become valleys and
Satan himself retreats to the dark regions of the abyss in the
onslaught of truth and righteousness. We should never fear
a barrier; we should never fear a challenge and we should

---

[47] 1 Nephi 3:7
[48] Alma 5:15

ever be vigilant in pursuing excellence in all that we do. *After all, we are children of God!*

SECTION 3

(Fragile maturity)

A common level of understanding
for
The young adult

We have this all figured out, right?
With young adulthood come the biggest decisions of life
including marriage and children. Let's discuss a few
concepts that each in this condition face.

Truth, Common #: 15
   Marriage is essential in our
   progression toward understanding

THE NEW AND EVERLASTING COVENANT

In a previous book, I outlined an experience I had years ago while on a backpacking trip on the Philmont Scout Reservation in Cimarron, New Mexico.[49]
The book was written for a broad audience and not necessarily for members of the church. The experience had a profound impact on me as I recognized it as something special, a gift from "the other side." I knew it was for a significant reason with implications and messages that was intended to reach far beyond me. The depth and width of the message was much greater than my ability to

---

[49] All of the Answers are in the Woods, We have friends there,
(A lesson from Mt. Phillips)

understand or communicate to others. Since that time, I have asked myself, and the Lord in prayer, how I was to share this precious and sacred message to others. I was not a writer, nor did I ever consider myself to be capable of being one.

It was not until decades later that I began to write about a few specialized topics and then began to understand that this was the medium intended for the delivery of the message. Therefore, I present to you the story as outlined in the book previously mentioned, followed by *the real story!*

The peace and challenge of backpacking seemed to be just the right combination. It allowed me to be in the woods but challenged me physically and provided emotional relief at the same time. We had been on the trail for eight days in a place called Philmont, in Cimarron New Mexico. It was early the next morning that we left wild horse campsite after a long night of cold and rain. Just before sunset, we stood in the small mountain meadow watching the lighting in the distance strike in colors as it was filtered through the humid atmosphere. It was a glorious evening but time to move on now for another segment along our 75 mile journey in the southern section of the reservation. With the early departure we were destined to reach Mt Phillips early in the day. At 11,711 feet above sea level, its summit offers few trees to offer resistance to the flow of upper atmosphere air currents which travel across it, yet we were anxious to arrive to enjoy the majesty of the views and to relish in the accomplishment of summiting the second highest peak on the reservation.

It appeared however, that the elements of the earth were none to anxious for us to arrive. As we approached the base of the mountain trail the torrential rain began. The farther we ascended, the colder it became and the rain soon turned to hail. There were few "switch backs" (cris-crossing) on the north end trail but the "frontal assault" (straight up) was the menu of the day. As the trail ascended straight up the face of the mountain, we would steady our climb by hanging onto the trees. They ascended straight toward the heavens but at a 45 degree to the earth beneath us.

Even though we were all well protected against the rain by ponchos, the moisture ascended from our bodies at a rate rivaling the descending rains. The sweat saturated every strand of clothing we had on making us wet from top to bottom. No problem, I thought, as long as we keep on moving we will be warm, "this cold ain't nothing!" As the summit came into view in the distance, the trees became less prevalent yielding to rocks and bushes. It was then that all four extremities were necessary to propel the tattered body the final steps. A flag pole graced the top sporting the stars and stripes standing at attention as the winds crossed at thirty knots.

121

It was a glorious site, with unrestricting views over the country side in nearly every direction. We took off our packs to take in the view, take pictures and to revel in our accomplishment. We had made it to the top of Mt Phillips! The exhilaration lent itself to concern as I was feeling the first signs of hyperthermia setting in. The stiff and unrelenting wind had taken its toll on our bodies. The core temperature was beginning to drop and all of the symptoms were setting in.

"Ok, let's go," I thought, "let's get out of this wind." I found some cover and climbed in my small tent. The rain had picked up again and was drenching as I descended a little bit off the face and into some adjoining trees on the leeward side. Setting up camp in the rain is never any fun and in emergency cold conditions, it is hazardous. Being warm and dry is key. I stripped off all of my wet clothes and to get into the sleeping bag. It was critical that stop the symptoms from progressing any further. Considering where we were, it would be a real problem to have to make an emergency extraction for a sick boy scout.

As they all followed my instructions, we settled in for what was going to be a very long day. Normally, the afternoon after reaching our camp site was filled with typical teenage frivolity and good natured mischief until they all lost the will to continue and surrendered to the fatigue earned by the days grind. Things would be different today. In our haste to conquer the mountain we had arrived just after lunch and then clamored up in our small portable shelters staring at the layer of nylon which protected us from the elements merely inches from our eyes.

"Well, it's OK," I thought. "We can do this, besides we have no other choice. This is the hand nature had dealt us today and we will play it." As I lay there staring up from my makeshift pillow, I remembered something: I have always told my kids that nature gives the greatest gifts to those who pay the highest price. We had witnessed something wonderful. We were occupying sacred ground. Mt Phillips would not give up its treasures easily but once you climbed it, the prize was priceless.

I left the tent to be sure that all of the boys had complied with my instructions and were doing ok and then returned to my own for the long wait. "I hope it is not like this all day, this is going to get real boring," I thought. As the minutes and hours passed I obviously drifted off to sleep. What happened during that time has changed my life in a very profound way ever since. I had a dream.

I have always heard stories about my grandfather. My mom would call him "Dad." In my years as a young man, my mom would always have a smile on her face as she told me about her dad. He was a man of stature both physically and spiritually. He worked all of his life in the steel mills near Birmingham, Alabama. He was loved and respected by all of those who had the privilege of associating with him. On his 50 year of service to the Mill, he was awarded a small pendent by the company. My grandmother gave it to me when I was young saying that Dad would want me to have it.

I have no memory of my grandfather. My family left Birmingham for the Atlanta area when I was a toddler under the protests of Dad. Mom told me that Dad had teased her that if they took little Andy away that we would die. Such idle threats are common among grandparents. I have said it a few times myself to my daughters who grace it with the same reaction as my mom did, she smiled at him, kissed his cheek and continued down life's road, which lead to Atlanta.

I do not know how much longer it was but I am told that it was shortly after that time that Dad passed away. All that he has ever been to me since then was a fond image of a very kind and loving man.

It was in a cramped tent on the top of Mt Phillips under pouring freezing rain that I met my grandfather (dad) for the first time. It was in the dream that I was standing alone in a mist. Approaching me were two men. One of them was my grandfather. Even though I had never seen him in eyes that I could recall, I recognized him instantly. No introductory words were spoken but I knew who he was. My impression at the time was that he was coming to "take me home." Recognizing the unearned rudeness of my greeting, I turned away and awoke in a sudden display of alarm.

I do not know how long it had been since I first fell asleep but the rain had stopped and the wind had waned a bit. Ignoring all cautions, I exited the tent in haste and walked to the summit in scant clothing. The events had such a profound impression as to make me believe that my time on the earth was very limited and that I would not be so lucky to escape their approach next time. I knew that I was little hypothermic but not that much. I had much experience with this on the trail and had felt that it was under control, but the events which took place could not be denied. Possibly I would not survive the night.

Finding a rock couch built by the ever industrious scouts, I sat to admire the landscape. Majesty and beauty displayed in glorious color, sights and sounds. A mountain rodent we called "mini bears" was going about his business in the nearby rocks and the hawks were riding the thermals as they pierced the canopy below for sustenance. Surely, there was no better place to spend my last days on earth.

The wind did not seem to sting as bad as before. It was just as cool but pleasant. The still present moisture against my skin and wind in my face would be the instrument used by nature to return my body to the earth. It was interesting that fear was not present; not in any way, but a spirit of reverence and respect for the mighty purposes of my maker that filled my heart and mind. I think I will stay here for as long as there is light in the sky, I thought, and then go to sleep where surely I will meet Dad again.

It was after some time that others in the camp began to stir. Weary from "tent fever" my friend Rich came to find me in the stone couch looking into eternity. "Andy, what the heck are you doing out here, don't you know that you could die out here?" After hearing the unknowingly prophetic question, I took inventory of my senses to determine if this experience was in fact real or another dream. Making light of my apparent foolish conduct, I invited Rich to have a seat, "Man, this view is awesome," I said. After making the customary small talk regarding the events of the day, we later retired to our bags for the night. With quiet reservation, I thought, surely this will be my last.

Morning came as usual. With accepting spirits to face an extension of my destiny, I packed up and left with the dawn. Never had I seen such a beautiful sunrise. With the view shared by larks and eagles I soaked it in and descended down the trail for another day. Three more days followed on the trail. Each day, I expected the inevitable, but each day I woke to my surprise. Having accepted my fate, it was almost frustrating that every day issues of life continued.

Keeping the experience to myself, I reached base camp on the fourth day. The telephone was the first thing to find. I need to hear the voice of my sweet wife. I was nearly 2000 miles from home; surely a hazard on the road would deliver the anticipated end. Hearing her voice was nothing like anything I had ever heard before.

Surely I had heard her sweet voice a million times a million times before, but it was as if I had just heard it for the first time in mortality. The years that had passed between my birth to then seemed like an instant between the veil and mortality. Yes I had heard that voice before; however, it was not here, it was from *before.* It was then that I knew that I had known her before coming here to earth. Whether we had made a commitment to each other was unclear, but I knew that she was a friend and that I had loved her there. Here we are, on earth as an eternal companionship.

It seemed unnecessary to alarm the other passengers in the car. My fate was my own. I was the anticipated target for recall, surely they would be spared. Each passing car was another respite from anticipated execution of the extraction order. The miles passed and the earth passed ever so slowly under the tires of the vehicle destined for home.

In the passenger's seat, I reached for the glove box. "Rich" I asked, "I need a pen and some paper. I have something to write down. If I lose it, please give it to Karen (my wife). Figuring that would be the only way she would receive it, I began to write. The words came with conviction and assuredly. I made a list of things figuring that I would understand it later. Uncertain how it would benefit anyone, I knew only that I had to write it down, and I did.

I did make it home and in fine condition. I have often thought what significance the experience could be. Was it for me or for someone else? The experience for me has taken on a new meaning as I have come to mature since then. What I have come to understand is that my grandfather was not coming to *get me* but he was delivering a message. In order to be prepared to receive it, I had to face my mortality, draw close to the veil, even the edge of life. Could this be where the angels live to help us though our trials of life?

The message delivered to me by my grandfather that day from "the other side of the veil" was one of comfort and peace. As I have struggled to receive the meaning of my life, I have come to understand that there are those who are watching us from a distance and caring for our happiness and success. It was a feeling of love and support which was overwhelming to the extent that no offences offered by man could dilute it. God is part of our everyday lives more than I could have ever imagined. This gift from the "other side" is one I will never forget.

Now, the rest of the story.........

In the preface of the book previously mentioned, I began by saying, "There is *something* out there! When I am surrounded by the beauty of the earth, I feel the presence of God Himself. Its beauty and harmony are proof and testament that He lives and that He loves us and has created a wonderful place for us. I have always felt His presence in these places among the hills, trees, forest and streams. This is where I have found *home* and retreat there often to hear his voice and to receive answers.

As I awoke from the *dream* that afternoon on the top of Mt Phillips, I realized what had just happened. It was not a dream but a divinely delivered message from someone I once knew and loved. I was certain of the message and the content but unsure of its purpose. The spiritual encounter figuratively took me to the doors of the eternal world so that I could be prepared to receive the message from beyond the veil. Over the next few days, I received a stream of thoughts which I scratched down on slips of paper I would find on the floorboard, or the glove box of the car. Certain, that I would not make it home, I asked my friend to be sure my wife received them.

It was not until several years later that I understood some of what happened. Obviously, I misinterpreted the event. My Grandfather had not come to *take me home.* He came to deliver a message and in order for me to be spiritually prepared to receive it, I had to be brought to the edge of where the earth meets heaven. I mistakenly believed that there would be no return.

For years following that, I wondered, why? Why would such a specific message of broad subject matter be delivered to such an undeserving subject as me? Well, the answer to that question remains elusive still. However, in an effort to attempt to feebly meet the challenge of sharing the message to my Brothers and Sisters in the Gospel I present the message content to you in its unfiltered form in the following paragraphs.

The message was very personal in one sense but also very broad in another. The overall subject was temple marriage, or the New and Everlasting Covenant. Here is the message word for word as it was written on the cumulative scraps of paper:

- The World will forever be different with this knowledge
- Water flowing from open breasts showing generations of people
- Marriage is not a purpose but THE purpose
- No longer faith but knowledge of the eternal nature of marriage
- Spouse and I have always known and loved each other since before the world was.
- Her voice is the physical manifestation of the spiritual being I once knew, heard only in mortality.
- Husband and wife are Co-Creators with God (a shared responsibility)
- Spouse is "Flesh of Flesh" and "Bone of Bone"
- The Physical Relationship is:
  - "Given unto thee"
  - No dishonor of body of other nor for self but for partner.
  - Is the physical manifestation of spiritual bond to each other?
  - Freely given for love and bonding to other: the guiding rule:
  Chastity before, Fidelity after
- Our marriage:
  - Was our mission

- Is to be an example to others
- Should be built
- Should be reverenced as a temple

- The spouse is the spiritual companion in bodily form. Every second should be shared with each other, as everyone is precious.
- Spirit children will come by a physical union of eternal couple, though process is perfected...........eternal happiness.
- The New and Everlasting Covenant seals and binds, holds together through faithfulness.
- Cannot stand to be separated, not even for a moment.
- We are one unto God. When separated we are partial, incomplete.
- Spouse is purpose of life and without her life goes away, figuratively.
- After a long separation, the voice contact shows how the loss of connection affects the spirit.
- Hear voice of (angel) and life begins to return
- Cling unto her and none other.
- Unity of this knowledge between the partners and understanding it builds unity knowing that obedience to Gods plan brings about the reality of these promises.
- It is all very real and wonderful.
- Marriage and Family is Center of the Gospel.
- The best thing you can do for your kids is to love your spouse and to have a successful marriage.

- Husband's primary responsibility is to build up wife, support her, and love her as a partner with God.
- Man cannot go alone: "neither wife without the man" or man without the wife before God.
- Know that a successful marriage will be a target. The foundation to which others will fall if shaken. This is effective targeting of the enemies.

Tools to build a successful marriage:

- Shared experiences
- Common goals and interests
- Respect and courtesy toward each other.
- How can I change MYSELF to improve my marriage?
- In the physical relationship there should be excitement (passion)
- Keep the love alive (with Honor and with reverence to what it represents).
- It involves only two people. It can be whatever you choose.

Enemies to Marriage

- Pride
- Selfishness
- Power Struggles
- Control Issues

- Unrighteousness Dominion
- Unreasonable Expectations of Partner
- Harmful Comparisons (Why can't you be like..?).
- Spiritual Differences (Testimonies and Standards).
- Child rearing (Differences in opinions).
- Differences in standards (Level of Obedience)

Over the years, I have looked at this list over and over again wondering what I should do with it. There were several answers that were personal and direct that was not outlined that dealt with prayers offered many times, seeking guidance from the Father.

There is one thing I have come to know with a certainty regarding the subject: we have no capacity to understand the magnitude of the beauty and joy that eternally await those who enter into and keep the sacred covenant of The New and Everlasting Covenant. In a small way, I witnessed the majesty of it and want to shout to the world to be careful to do whatever is necessary to be worthy of this blessing when we *reach the other side.*

It is however important to point out, that this blessing will be made available to all those who live worthy of it and seek for it in their heart whether or not they have had an opportunity to participate in it in mortality. The Lord is perfect in His wisdom and mercy.

Because marriage and family is the center of the Gospel plan, it is the prime target for the destroyer. He will attack marriage as an institution, a concept, idea or tradition. He will even attack one's sense of sexual orientation as a distraction because he knows that when marriages and families break down so does society and civilization and when those things break down, there is misery, just like his. This is his goal and part of the opposition we face in mortality.

Having a small insight into this magnificent blessing, I am amazed at the love Heavenly Father must have for us to make this unthinkable blessing possible for us. It is truly, to be like God, Him, to create, to grow to have eternal progression and posterity. *"For behold, this is my work and my glory, to bring to pass the immortality and eternal life of man."*[50]

This is the pinnacle of gifts from the Father. There is nothing greater or more precious. He knows this and freely gives through the power of the atonement and the plan of salvation. Great blessings require great obedience. In order to receive this great gift, we must prove to be worthy of it. The consequence of obedience is joy and happiness.

The tradeoff is obviously unfair in our favor. Why would we ever find the terms of the payment difficult to accept? It all seems pretty simple to me!

---

[50] Moses 1:39

Truth, Common #16:

The process of raising children will help you "understand."

THE POWER OF PARENTING

Some of the most sensitive memories of our lives are imprinted on our hearts and minds in the earliest years of our lives. Being delivered to the earth in an innocent and helpless condition, being totally dependent on our caregivers, we learn the necessities for survival through motor skills and cognitive reasoning. Inherently, we love and admire our parents. With infant tongues unable to form words and un-imprinted minds unable to develop reason, we trustingly submit ourselves to others controlling our immediate destiny.

Somewhere along the way, our minds are capable of recording sounds, sights and smells. These physical impressions are filtered through thought and reason to develop impressions and opinions. As we grow to acquire and accumulate diverse stimuli, our processing center (the mind) improves its ability to distinguish their differences and determine which feels good and which feels bad.

The psyche of a child is self-absorbed. Not able to look far beyond themselves, their world is limited and small to equal their concept of themselves as compared to the infinite world before them. As their bodies begin to grow and mature, they sense another influence within them...the spirit.

Many that walk the trails of life on the planet earth are unable to distinguish between the two entities, body and spirit. The real divergence occurs in the process of explaining the origins and destiny of these entities. This divergence can be channeled by belief systems carried on by tradition or culture. They can be individually taught by trusted caregivers and adopted as fact. Regardless of where we are planted in the soil of mortality, we are all spiritual beings embodied in flesh and blood made from the elements of the earth, an earthly tabernacle of clay.[51]

Many are planted in well-kept gardens where they can grow to the extent of their capabilities while others are left to grow in rocky soil left alone to survive with whatever nourishment they can acquire. At times, it seems random in the selection process but we know that the Lord is infinite in His wisdom and nothing is random. There is a place for each of us, divinely appointed. We may not know the reasoning until we *leave the game* but we know that He

---

[51] Mosiah 3:8

is our father and He does have a purpose in all that He does.

Within the earthly garden, there are parents who carefully prepare the soil, gently plant the seed and anxiously await the new sprout to emerge from the fertile soil. They water it, pull the weeds from its stem and support its outstretched branches when needed. They cover the tender plants when it is cold and protect it from the damaging sun and heat when it becomes harsh. The fruit is borne with satisfaction to the gardener and the plant as it has filled the measure of its creation.

In contrast, consider the plant that is tossed in the wind to find suitable soil by chance or coincidence. The seed fights against the odds to burrow into the inhospitable soil. It forces its expansion into the crust by overcoming adversity at every turn. As the weeds who have long occupied the spot refuse access, the little seed strengthens its roots to provide the upward pressure necessary to overcome the relentless resistance.

Having no other option but to live or die, the little seed gains strength through little nourishment. This strength is used to move outward and upward. It eventually overcomes its oppressors and demands its own allotment of ground created by God Himself.

Although the fruit is similar from the two plants, their experience in preparing for the process is very different. This is similar to our life experiences in a distinctive way.

Being raised in the Church, I have seen plants who have emerged to produce fruit from all types of soil. Some were tender and pliable while others were tough and unbendable in their resolve. I have always known what type of plant I was and where I came from but continued to question, why?

In our early years, the question usually goes unanswered but we trudge along, expecting the answers to come later. In some cases the answers do come but in most they do not. It is not that the questions have not been answered, but that we could not *hear* or understand the transmitted message.

My dad was a good man. He had a good heart and a strong testimony of the Gospel. He took me to church and allowed and encouraged my understanding of the Gospel message. He was raised in rocky soil and was shaped by hardship to become a strict disciplinarian with little understanding on parenting or the skills necessary to raise emotionally balanced children.

The days turned into years as I struggled with feelings of rejection, failure and even betrayal. I would hold my hand up to the passing sky to simulate an aircraft as I lay on the rear seat of our family sedan and fly, fly away to my dreams. The hand would dip and climb through the clouds, make high speed turns and travel at mach speeds eluding even the most worthy adversary. Faster than anyone, I would be free to survey the heavens at my will, free to determine my direction and destiny, but later in life; I wondered how life could have turned out so differently than what I had hoped for as a boy.

One day led to another. They came in succession that would lead to the accumulating blocks that would become the foundation of my life. Even though I found love and support at a young age by a loving and caring companion, she was unable to understand the chemistry in my life that makes it difficult to manage.

It is funny how the earliest memories of childhood have such profound impact on the balance of our lives. Although we can eventually physically break free of its grips we are forever captive to the stains of ink indelibly etched in our memory.

The thoughts of a child are precious. They trust, love and respect those that care for them; they are everything, the ones that conceived and sustained their lives. This reality is constantly paraded across our minds eye as we review our station in life and our placement on this earth. We become the sum of life's experiences. Degrading comments to children reside in their minds like a cancer to their sense of worth and potential.

Through the uses of procreative functions (responsible or not) we enter the fabric of life as a helpless child and *grow where we are planted*. As we become aware of our surroundings, we witness behavior, conduct and consequences which we are free to observe and to learn from.

It is from the concept of "line upon line, precept upon precept" that we learn and grow.[52] This is a predictable and understandable process, where we can use our intellect to make decisions and to direct our path

---

[52] Ish 28:10

forward. It is the process where of great learning can be accomplished for the benefit of society and mankind.

Once the spirit becomes the filter of the stimulus of life, real progress can be made. Through all of the challenges however, I have always known that the Lord was cognizant of me. The youthful temptations fell unfulfilled as I felt His watchful eyes upon me. I know now that it was the spirit inside me that *knew* my Father in Heaven. It was this whispering that directed my life, no matter what circumstances I faced. This recognition of the spirit is the key to success in the lives of all of us, especially as a child.

As parents and caregivers, we should always be aware of this truth and never do anything to distract from this objective. The spirit is inseparably connected to the body, from an eternal perspective and the only sure earthly companion to show us the way.

The *evolutionary* process is alive and well in the hands of the Lord as we grow and progress through time, one thought and experience built upon another. May we always be instruments in the hand of the Lord to plant and nurture His garden so the fruit will be pleasing to Him to build His kingdom.

Truth, Common #17:
  It takes a while to understand the
  true nature of obedience.

AM I DOING THIS RIGHT?

Most of my professional life has been spent working with people as they dealt with financial risk. Insurance was not the most glamorous profession but it gave me the opportunity to be with my family when needed, serve in the church and to control my own schedule. Any position where your livelihood depends on constant performance such as sales generates a lot of stress which takes a toll on one's psyche. In an effort to subdue its effects, I would spend my lunch period across the street in the local gym.

  On one such occasion, after I changed and began my routine, I noticed a woman studying the configuration of a weight machine next to me. She operated the leverage mechanism with some degree of uncertainty and with a small tone of frustration in her voice; she turned towards me and asked a direct question, "Am I doing this right?" After a small amount of instruction she continued with the exercise and moved on.

Even though I have never seen her since, her question has played on my mind many times since, "Am I doing this right?" As you walk into any good gym and look around, you see many things. Mostly, it is stacks of metal, specifically designed and shaped to fit on bars that can be lifted, pulled, pushed, curled, swung, pressed and dropped. These weights vary from very light to very heavy. Treadmills, ellipticals, and stair masters are there along with stationary bicycles.

Every piece of equipment is designed for one thing: to **provide resistance**! Resistance is specifically designed for application to a specific muscle group. Depending on how the resistance is applied, different parts of the body will be affected.

It is in this practical application that we come to understand the workings of the Lord as He teaches us in 2 Nephi 2:11,

> *"For it must be, that there is an opposition in all things. If not so, my first born in the wilderness, righteousness could not be brought to pass, neither wickedness, neither holiness nor misery, neither good nor bad. Wherefore, all things must needs be a compound in one; where, if it should be one body it must needs remain as dead, having no life neither death, nor corruption nor incorruption,*

happiness nor misery neither sense nor insensibility. "

The words of the scripture describe a "total body workout" but in a spiritual sense, *"all things to the Lord are spiritual. "*[53] Just as each movement in the gym isolates specific muscle groups, each layer of resistance in our lives builds spiritual muscle.

Every weightlifter knows that the only reason he is able to lift the weight he can is because he started with the smaller ones. He pushed and pulled it until it was no longer heavy so he graduated to the next level of weight. He then repeated the process until his mind was in control. His mind told his body he could do it, and he did! After a period of dedication to this process, amazing things are accomplished. Only after limits were reached and overcome can the next level of strength be obtained. Eventually, you will become stronger than you ever thought you could be.

This is a natural process. Why then is it harder for so many of us to understand that there is "no other way" to build spiritual muscle. The Lord built our bodies; He understands these principles.

As you consider the circumstances in your life, children, family and neighbors, it is easy to understand how they can be specifically designed and shaped to apply resistance to your life. As you learn to overcome this resistance you become stronger. If we are to become like

---

[53] D&C 29:36-39

Him, we must face these challenges. This was part of the original plan and why we are here.

At times the weight seems too heavy, more than we can bear. When this would happen to me in the gym, there were two options, dropping it or keep trying. Now, the message may be different here than what you may think. I am sure you would expect the counsel to be to keep trying no matter what until you succeed.

Well, that was my attitude until I got tired of visits to the hospital, chiropractors and various doctors to help me deal with the pain resulting in trying to do something outside my physical capabilities. The result was usually torn muscles, broken bones and ligaments that take months or even years to heal setting back any advance I may have made in the muscle building process.

This "can do at any cost" mentality can be counterproductive and defeat the original purpose. We should be sensible in our approach and not try to take on more than we can bear. Understanding that sometimes the level of our "application of resistance" is out of our control, we need to always have someone to help us. Help may take many forms, shapes and varieties.

Whenever we try to push beyond our level of comfort in the gym we ask for a "spotter." This is someone who stands behind you to help if needed. This backup person gives you comfort knowing that if it becomes too heavy, he will be there to keep you from getting hurt.

We have a spiritual spotter in our lives. He is Jesus Christ. He will always be there when the weight becomes too heavy. With this level of comfort, we are able to pursue greater and greater amounts of resistance that none could exceed His abilities for assistance. We need many spotters in our lives. They can be a spouse, family members or good friends.

The doctrine of Christ is the basis for all spiritual strength and sufficient to accelerate us to the most impressive spiritual body one can build on this earth. Practice of the doctrine is the muscle power that makes all the weight in the world light to us. No amount of opposition the world can deliver will negate the fact that Jesus is the Christ and that He stands as a redeemer and advocate with the father. One early apostle tells us, *"for my yoke is easy and my burden is light."*[54]

Because we are in this world, it is certain that we will have burdens. We will have yokes upon our necks; it is unavoidable and you will face opposition. To the extent we are able to bear it depends on our ability to *push back* with the strength we have acquired. We can take comfort in the fact that the Lord will permit us to have more opposition than we are able to bear.[55]

As much as we see opposition all around us, there are equally (if not more) solutions, answers and comfort. They may come in the ways possibly unfamiliar to us but they are there all the same. In the end we can answer the original question by asking ourselves these questions:

- Am I on the right path?
- Am I holding on to the Iron Rod?

---

[54] Matt 11:30
[55] Joseph B. Wirthland 1989

- Am I doing the thing the Lord has asked to do?

If these simple questions are answered to the affirmative, we can truly say that no matter how far we are on the path of life, we are... "Doing this right!"

Truth, Common #: 18
We must learn how Distraction can be used as a very effective tool against us.

DISTRACTION

It is on occasion that each of us, at one point or another, has the privilege to participate in our democratic process and serve on a jury of our peers in our communities. I had this opportunity some years ago, but it was not my first. Because of my profession, I was always removed from the acceptable pool of jurors because of my "training" in the law. That fact always seemed curious to me as it would appear that they choose those unfamiliar with the process.

Nearing the end of the day and in an apparent desperate attempt to fill the jury, I was assigned to a case with little to no personal questions. It was a case where a gentleman was accused of driving while under the influence of alcohol. It was a simple case really, where the prosecution presented the case of how the accused was caught by a county police officer noticing erratic driving and that his blood alcohol level was twice the legal limit when he was submitted to a field sobriety test.

However, when the defense attorney began questioning the police witness and presenting his case, the facts were the least of his concerns. "Are you an officer of the Law?" his questioning began. "Yes, I am," he replied. "Are you a member of the Drunk Driver Task Force?" he continued. Again his response was a simple "yes." "So you admit that you were deliberately out on the street that night looking for drivers you could pull over." The police officer skillfully replied, "It is my job to look for drivers who may pose a threat to the public, and I identified this driver as a potential risk due to his erratic driving."

As the defense attorney continued along this stream of questioning in an attempt to label the officer as one who entrapped his client, he later concentrated on the details of the field sobriety tests. "So what kind of game did you force my client to play," he demanded. The officer outlined the standard test to have a person display balance by standing on one leg and counting backwards from ten. This disclosure excited the attorney as he attempted to perform the physical exercise in the courtroom. While standing on one foot and bouncing up and down, he turned to the jury and comically asked, "Can any of you do this?" insinuating that the task was unreasonable for anyone to perform.

His attention then turned to the injustice of the law enforcement system who would detain a citizen of the community from going about his legally allowed freedom of movement after only having "one beer" in a local tavern. Curiously, I watched as the wrangling continued for the defense until it was at last turned over to the jury for a decision.

There only being six of us assigned, we entered the deliberation room and took our seats. I sat quietly as those around me discussed the things we heard and took the defense up on his challenge to perform the "one legged hop" maneuver. "You know, this is really hard," one of them replied. Not believing what I was witnessing, I took control of the discussion to make a point. "You know, there are only two things to decide here. The question we have to answer is was his blood alcohol limit above the legal limit and was he driving? Everything else is irrelevant."

Surprisingly, they seemed to agree with the logic (after some discussion) and we continued with a hasty conviction. He was twice the legal limit, and yes, he was driving…end of discussion.

It was interesting to me that in absence of favorable facts, the accused will always throw out distractions to curb our attention away from the details. In the military, they are called countermeasures, diversions or dummy drones, anything to direct the aggression of the enemy to targets that are not real.

The facts of the restored gospel are that Jesus in the Christ. He and God the Father appeared to the boy Prophet Joseph Smith in a grove in upstate New York in the year 1820 and that through him the Book of Mormon was translated and the fullness of the Gospel was restored to the earth. These are the only relevant facts that apply to our search for truth on this planet.

Those who oppose the church and seek to turn the sons and daughters of man away from its eternal truths throw out distractions to blind their path. There will be talk of the early history of the church. There will be diaries, stories, testimonials and sworn documents from those supposedly in the *know* that discredit people and events but there will never be invalidation of the first vision or the divinity of the Book of Mormon; other than those things all other discussions are irrelevant.

Distraction is the smoke that obscures your path. In the process of reacquiring your course, you look down or look back. In that moment, the enemy will place an obstacle in your way to trip you as you begin to regain your forward momentum. As you pick yourself off the ground, your perspective is momentarily lost and you must take valuable time to assess your situation and desired direction. In the process, you have stopped your forward motion and are now briefly stationary to gather your thoughts and determination. In that moment you are vulnerable for attack and redirection.

In my younger life, I attended college at night while working during the day. It took me ten years of night school to finish my Bachelors degree at a University located in downtown Atlanta. I would pass several street corners on my way from the parking lot to the campus where I would often come into contact with those asking for money. Often, they would simply want to engage me in conversation regarding their personal plight in the world and the injustices that were responsible for their demographic placement.

To engage one of these individuals in conversation would be a guarantee of bewilderment in logic and sensibilities. By the time you were ready to proceed with your pace, you would have to overcome considerable reasoning with an unreasonable person and wishing you had never become involved. The only conclusion to render is that the temporary halt in forward motion was a distraction that served no valuable purpose.

Once we come to know what direction we need to go and what we need to accomplish is determined, any deviation from the appointed path is a distraction that may serve no valuable purpose. Once we acquire a knowledge of the restored gospel and we take of the new and everlasting covenant, there is nothing but a motion of forward and onward that will serve to accomplish our goal to endure to the end.

The fact that there is a good and bad, right and wrong or sin or righteousness is diluted for the argument of tolerance and acceptance of others *differences*. Distractions then become the norm to turn us away from the path we were originally set upon. Those who first took hold of the iron rod became distracted as they heard the mocking voices of those from the great and spacious building. They turned, lost their way in the fog and fell into the river.

It does not matter what "he said, she said." All that matters is that the church is true. Nothing else matters! However, in the frivolity of life and the enticements that serve as distractions, the enemy of all righteousness will throw distractions our way in an effort to have us loose our focus on what is important. By jumping up and down on one leg he may say, "Look how hard it is to be good all of the time. I bet you cannot do it. You should not be expected to follow any commandments because you are *free* to exercise your *rights* and you should be able to "do what you want."

Distractions should be treated as such, dismissed as harmful to our forward motion. Though they are a powerful tool in the hands of a skilled adversary, they can have no effect on us if we stay focused on our mission. Distractions are a very effective weapon; stay focused, stay on mission and leave the distractions to the homeless and bitter naysayers. That is where they belong.

Truth, Common #: 19
  The Lords perspective is usually
  very different than ours.

IF YOU ONLY KNEW

It is never a surprise to me when it happens, but it also never fails to amaze me how the Lord has control of His kingdom and knows when and how to do things. Truly, His prospective is eternal.

I was called to serve as a Branch President of a small branch in the South. We were a typical small branch with barely enough faithful saints to do the necessary tasks. The concept of "STP" was alive and well. We jokingly used this acronym to stand for the "same ten people." They were the same ones that would always seem to do everything. The youth group was tiny with my daughter being one of the only young women in the unit. The spirit was strong there and we seemed to get along just fine.

After a year or so, the unit grew just enough to make it a ward, just barely.

This was the condition we found ourselves in when we received a visit from a General Authority. He was there to investigate the possibility of forming a new stake in the area that would include several units from a neighboring stake and our little ward. My first counselor was raised in the proposed new stake area and was familiar with the units considered. "Bishop," he said to me, "I know those units. They are very small and the ones that are wards are not very strong. I don't see how this could work." As a matter of fact, considering the units discussed, our unit was one of the strongest of the ones considered. I thought, we are doing ok, but we barely have enough to meet our own needs, much less to provide priesthood to help run a new stake. The meeting was short and sweet and afterward, I marveled at the possibility that at some point in the very distant future, this could be a possibility.

Well, it wasn't in the distant future. As a matter of fact, it was less than two years later that the new Stake was organized. It is in this experience and countless others like it that the Lord teaches us that He is in charge. He knows when things need to happen and where. He has perspective that we lack, not just in the organization of His church but in our lives as well. He can see our soul and knows its potential. He sees who we are and more importantly what we can become.

Having some memory of my childhood days, I recall a certain young man with the self-image of a" super hero." When the bully would pick on him he would warn,

"Man you better not mess with me. You have no idea who you are dealing with.... IF YOU ONLY KNEW! Wouldn't it be wonderful if we could know of ourselves the way the Lords knows of us; knowing what we are and what we can become?

On one summer evening years ago my family was on an outing on one of those Saturday afternoons that are fondly labeled in the Deep South as "dog days." We decided that a visit to the nearest ice cream parlor would be just the thing. While we were standing at the counter receiving our treats, I saw a car pull up. Immerging were several young women in their early teens. I saw one young woman particularly leap from the car with great enthusiasm. The joyful anticipation of the cool and tasty treat was written on her beautiful little face.

I could tell in an instant that she was a choice daughter of God and that He loves her very much. Through the spiritual gifts given me as a servant of our heavenly father, I could see her sweet spirit and the many great things she could accomplish. However, as she came closer, I could see the piercing and tattoos that dishonored her body. The spirit fell to disappointment as it was clear that this young woman ....Did not know.....*who she was or what she could become*. "If you only knew," were the words I heard in my head.

Before the Earth was, there was a grand council in heaven. All of the spirit children of God were gathered in countless numbers.[56] Spirits who were literal offspring of

---

[56] Mos 4:1

an eternal God who had potential power over the elements of the universe were gathered to consider a mortal experience.

We would come to earth, gain a body and be tested. Knowledge of our pre-existence would be taken from our mortal memory but it would pull at our spirits. Surely with this knowledge, we rushed forward to accept the challenge. We wanted to be like Heavenly Father, have eternal sons and daughters of our own and rule in our own kingdoms for time and eternity.

There was one of the great ones offering a guarantee: Give me thine honor and I will bring them all back. Having been thrown from God's presence for rebellion, it has been his mission ever since to have us fail in our quest. In our misery, he rejoices in a futile vindictive effort to justify his evil position. He will not prevail! Some will follow him, but they that do will be left behind to consider what they could have had, what they could have been and what they could have achieved; "Of all sad words of tongue or pen, the saddest of these are: It might have been."[57]

As a loving father looks upon his beautiful daughter, he sees her for what she can be and wants her to fulfill her potential. When Heavenly Father sends His sons and daughters here to earth, He depends on us as parents to teach them those things. Sadly, in most cases, that does not happen. Instead, they are taught the ways of the world and this was apparently the case with this young woman. She

---

[57] John Greenleaf Whittier 1807-1892

had been taught that it was "cool" to defile her precious body with ink and steel.

As a parent, and a leader it is our responsibility to teach the children the essential doctrine:

- They are children of God.
- They have eternal potential.
- Jesus Christ is their elder Brother.
- He took an earthly body and atoned for their sins.
- They can be Baptized, receive the blessings of the gospel and be happy.
- They can enter the Temple and receive the new and everlasting covenant of marriage that will endure through the eternities.
- They can return with their families intact: sons and daughters eternally.
- The Gospel in its fullness has been restored to the earth today.
- We have a living Prophet that will always teach us how to stay on the path of righteousness and will never lead us astray.

It is often said that kids do not come with instructions, or even a warranty; I agree completely. However, they came from the same place that we did. God delivered these spirits to us the same as we were delivered to our parents.

Parents are given the ability to see them for what they are and help them reach their potential. As the mother joins with God to bring life into the world, the feeling surely must be considered by her that the power to create life is larger than herself.

If you do not know who *you* are, you will not be in a position to teach that to your children. I suspect that the young woman I saw, came from a family that could not teach her the things we have discussed because they themselves have not been taught. So the tradition of unbelief and ignorance is perpetuated.

Such are the circumstances that foster an environment where children become worldly. They are in the world, they are taught by the world, they are influenced by worldly things and they become a product of the world. From what I see of the world today it is not something that brings happiness or joy.

True joy and happiness comes through obedience to the Gospel of Jesus Christ. We cannot be obedient to a law without knowing what the law is. Knowing the law, understanding its principles and covenanting to abide by its principles will bring great blessings. Herein we are promised to have all that the Lord has. There is no greater source of joy than to enjoy the doctrine of Christ and to participate in its fullness.

I believe we get in trouble when we take *ownership* of things that do not belong to us. For example: these kids do not belong to us. They are on loan from God. He has created this earth for the benefit of all of his children to reach their potential. We are instruments in His hands to teach the next generation of His children about *who they are and who they can become*. They do not belong to us.

We do however, have the right to claim them as ours if we live worthy of them in the eternal scheme of things but they are their own people with their own destinies. We will be held accountable to God in our roles as parents. I believe if we all understood and live by this principle; the world would be a much different place.

Truth, Common #: 20

The goals we have set for ourselves may not be the same as set by the Lord.

THE DESTINATION
MAY NOT BE
THE OBJECTIVE

You know, applying business principles to personal goals is not that difficult. It is all in the organization. First you figure out what you want to do. Then, you figure out the best way to get there. The route is carefully considered, weighing all the options, the plan is adopted and put in motion. It seems simple, but the best laid and perfectly executed plans sometimes just don't work out, sometimes not at all! I had done everything right, I thought. What I had thought to be a tragedy of fate was actually planned all along, just not by me.

Duke Porritt had lived a long and productive life and was now retired as a "full bird" Colonel from the

United States Air force. As a B17 pilot in WWII, Duke was shot down three times behind enemy lines, captured and held captive as a prisoner of war twice. It was difficult for the Germans to hold Duke for long however. He seemed to escape every time they caught him.

One time he was taken outside the POW compound to work on reinforcing the walls. Duke hid in the very hole he was tasked to dig. As the daylight began to fade, the guards gathered the prisoners to return with one less prisoner; that would be Duke Porritt. Duke would later unearth himself from the dirt and slip into the night to find his waiting compatriots.

Duke was a man of character and presence. He was "bigger than life," a man of great interest to those surrounding him. Because of his worldwide travels in the military and endless experiences in the various cultures of the world. Duke was a virtual treasure-trove of knowledge and wisdom on endless topics.

Duke was raised in the Church by a stalwart family, but allowed his military career to separate him from the constant fellowship necessary to maintain resistance to the relentless pressures of the world. He was however, always faithful to his beloved wife and high school sweetheart who suffered greatly because of his persistent pursuit of duty to county and the cause of the Allied Forces over Europe. Duke recalls saying, "Here we go again," as his bomber took enemy fire penetrating the fuselage (and his legs) as he occupied the pilot seat. Duke's wife knew her husband was in harm's way, and knew that he was captured (each time) but it was something she never got used to.

Retiring from the Air Force later in life, Duke settled in the small fishing community of Destin, Florida where he was close to the nearby Eglin Air Force Base and Hurlburt Field. His modest brick/ranch home was tastefully adorned with souvenirs accumulated as he served in command positions and administrator in various locations in Europe, Asia and the United States. A man of great duty, honor, respect, capability and knowledge was resting in the single family dwelling along with all the others of this small residential neighborhood.

The kids, all grown now have long since moved away to begin lives of their own. Scattered across the county engaged in their various professions, they stay in touch with mom and dad as needed but leave them to enjoy the balance of their lives protected from the horror of war and separation. Duke had served his country with honor and was now enjoying his life with his sweetheart and the quiet life on the sandy soil of the emerald coast on the Gulf of Mexico.

It was a day like any other when Duke Porritt woke to begin his day. Following his morning coffee and the read of the newspaper headlines, Duke responded to a knock on the door. As the front door swung open, the outline of a tall man dressed in a white shirt, suit and tie stood on the small concrete porch. Without introduction, the man held out his hand to engage in a friendly gesture and as he shook hands the stranger boldly said, "Duke it is time for you to get your life in order. The Lord has need of you." Following, the apparent direct instruction, the retired military line officer, familiar with the frankness of direct

162

instruction, engaged in light conversations and thanked the stranger for the visit.

The door was politely closed leaving Duke a moment to contemplate what had just happened. With his hand still on the door knob, moments following the exchange, Duke opened the door again to inquire how they had found him. Obviously, this man was a member of the church of his youth and has somehow found out he was living in the area. It was curious however, Duke had made no effort to make his presence known to the church. It was a mystery.

Seeing that the stranger had left the front stoop, Duke proceeded to the front yard expecting to see a vehicle so that he could inquire further, but the driveway was empty. "Certainly, he didn't have enough time to walk from my door, get in a car and leave in that amount of time," he thought. The yard, street and sidewalks were however, most definitely void of any presence. As strange as it appeared, Duke resolved himself to find the closest LDS congregation and make an appearance to congratulate the gentlemen for getting his attention. "Some of those home teachers can be pretty ingenious," he told himself. Dressing himself up, Duke passed over the threshold door of The Church of Jesus Christ of Latter-Day Saints for the first time in fifty years.

With this arrival, the Lord returned what would prove to be a valuable servant to the kingdom of God. Duke never saw that stranger at church that day nor any day following. As a matter of fact, the members of the Fort Walton 1st Ward had never heard of a man fitting that description, nor were they aware of Duke's residence in their boundaries. However, from that day forward, Duke devoted all of his waking hours to the building of the kingdom of God and was instrumental in the reactivation of an entire less active community of God. Duke became the executive secretary, Bishop and member of the Stake Presidency. His uncompromised leadership and magnetic personality began a wave of growth and activity unmatched by memory or experience.

I can say with all sincerity and honesty, that Duke Porritt was the most spiritually instrumental man to have ever influenced my life. I loved this man and drew great strength from him. The Lord knew where Duke was and what potential he represented. I know that the Lord reactivated him for the welfare of many of His sons and daughters but at times I believe that the stranger *commanded* Duke to return to the Lord's service because he knew that Andrew E. Jones was coming to his area and needed his influence desperately.

Arriving in Destin, Florida following my discharge from the United States Army as an emotional and physical train wreck: I was quickly taken in by this great man serving then as the Bishop. It would be over the next several years that Duke made an extraordinary effort to spend personal time with me to teach gospel details, to share in his life's experiences and his love for me. Looking back, I do not believe that there could have been any other man alive that had the combination of personal traits that could have provided the healing I needed. Duke was a *tender mercy* delivered to my figurative doorstep that set the foundation of leadership I have been called to fill since then. I can trace the progressionary path of my life that defined who I was and what I would become. It was under Dukes tutelage that I understood what leadership looked like and what it was intended to do.

Duke led by doing, not telling. He was the first to do the right thing and invite others to follow. He used his past as a strength to him rather than to allow it to haunt him as an image of lost opportunity. His life's experiences served him wonderfully as he was able to communicate and console others in a way he would have never been able to without such experiences. He did not apologize for his past. He used it as an example of how the world can lure us away from the most important things in life, and I loved him for it.

As our lives continue down the road toward eternity, Duke moved to Colorado Springs, Colorado with his companion and within a few years he quietly passed away. Serving as a Bishop at the time, I flew to the local ward to attend the service. I expected there not to be a facility large enough to house those that would attend, I found many open seats among the pews of the building. "Surely," I thought, "These people have no idea who Duke was." As the family lovingly asked me to say a few words at the service, I recalled a few choice experiences we had together. Standing at the pulpit above the casket containing Duke's body, I took one step back, snapped to attention and briskly raised my right arm to salute this man whom had I had known so briefly but who had had such a profound influence on my life.

Odd still, was the apparent convolution of "random events" that presented me to Duke's tutelage. In a seemingly catastrophic collapse of expected outcomes, my disfigured spirit was dropped at the doorstep of this friend with a stranger saying, *you are needed in the kingdom.* Duke heard and answered the call as should all of us.

We never know what the Lord has in store for us and what set of seemingly random events are perfectly orchestrated by the Master's hand to benefit in eternal measures. Our destiny is sometimes in the Lord's hand, we just need to give Him a chance to arrange it. It was only after Joseph Smith's father lost the family's wealth[58] that they were influenced to move to Palmyra where Joseph could find the plates and be an instrument in the hand of the Lord to restore the Church. We do not know nor can we tell what the Lord has in store; we only need to believe, have faith and maintain worthiness so that His will may be manifested in our lives.

I cannot speculate, nor did Duke speculate, who the stranger was (at least not openly). We only knew that he came, he was real and that he knocked on the door. The visit began a series of events that influenced many people for good. It was the Lord's work and He has servants. There are many such examples in the scriptures. Wouldn't the Lord use the same tools today as He has in the past?[59]

---

[58] The life of Joseph Smith the Prophet, George Q. Cannon, Desseret Books, 1986, pg.25,26

[59] Alfa and omega same today, yesterday and forever.

I believe the message from my experiences with my friend Duke is clear.

- Remember that the Lord loves you.
- He is aware of you and wants you to reach your potential.
- It is important to remain worthy so that the Lord can bless you.
- Do not ever second guess His promptings.

There are times that we think we have it all figured out. We pray, we receive answers and we follow the promptings. However, somewhere along the path, the train jumps the track. We believe we knew its destination but it never got there.

The destination was not the objective. He never said that we would reach our intended destination, He only told us to begin the journey.

Something was placed in its way and a derailment occurred, a disaster right? Well, no, not necessarily. At the accident scene there is a person, a place or an object we find that we would have never discovered unless we landed at that specific spot at that specific time. It took a train wreck to get us there.

This was the lesson I learned that has served me valuably since then and one we must apply to our lives. I would have never met Duke on my planned route; it necessitated a diversion. It was never a train wreck; I only perceived it to be. There is great healing in this understanding and a concept that delivers the methods of God to His children.

There will be places we need to be, people we need to meet and things we need to do. We have no way of knowing what they are; we are mortal and cannot extend our consciousness beyond our scope of knowledge or understanding. The Lord however, sees it all, the world and every person in it and all at the same time. He knows what we must do and who we must meet.

No mortal has this ability, only the Lord. He sends His servant's to further the work. Sometimes they come in the form of friends, family members, church leaders or teachers. However, in extreme circumstances and when necessary to fulfill His eternal purposes, He will send a stranger to YOUR door and remind you of a motto we had in the military…"You can run, but you cannot hide." …especially from the Lord! I can only imagine what kind of person Duke would have been if he had been in the Lord's service longer. The thought brings joy and sadness at the same time.

I look back and consider the possibilities. If my plans had totally succeeded and my diversion to Florida had not taken place, I would have never had the association with Bro Porritt. I believe now, that nothing I would have successfully achieved professionally could have compensated for the blessings of his fellowship. I did not know that then, but the Lord did. I know it now and am thankful that the Lord intervened in my life to bless me with this gift that will forever serve me in a positive way.

We should all consider the fact that if we remain worthy, the Lord will bless us. We may not understand it at the time but all things will reveal themselves in due time. After all, The God of Heaven and earth, is our Dad.

Truth, Common, #: 21
      There will always be trials,
      some may be very hard.

WHERE IS GOD?

As I have moved on from the professional world to the life I now lead, it has been a pleasure to establish a non-profit corporation dedicated to the effort of assisting communities before, during and after times of disaster. When entering these devastated areas, there may be many who ask the question, "Where is God?" Considering all of the devastation around them and seeing their life in turmoil, it is easy to understand why they would think such a thing. The question seems simple enough but I would suppose its basis stems from the lack of understanding.

Do they believe that God is a respecter of persons who protects them from trials or hardship? If so, why would a just and perfect God protect some and not all of his children? Does God, who is the Father of all of the children on earth, love some more than others? What about your own children; do you have a preference? Well of course in a lighter moment, we may answer yes to the latter question but in our hearts we know that the love we have for our children is equal, just different.

Each of our children have different personalities, characters, talents and traits that make them unique; it is the beauty of humanity. *"For behold, this is my work and my glory, to bring to pass the immortality and eternal life of man."*[60] In this scripture, he did not say *some of man.* As hard as it is to accept, trials and hardships are a part of life and how we face them defines who we are and what we are made of.

In our private and subconscious mind we may indulge such thought process and by so doing will be in prominate company. The prophet Joseph asked this question in Liberty Jail, *"Oh God where art thou? And where is the pavilion that covereth thy hiding place?"*[61] The prophet Lehi was caught murmuring when the bow of Nephi was broken and they were wanting for food.[62]

As we review the events in the world through the various news agencies, we hear of injustices of every kind, unspeakable crimes of man and nations. Countries are devastated by natural or manmade calamities leaving thousands or millions suffering physically, mentally and spiritually asking, "How could God allow such a thing to

---

[60] Moses 1:39
[61] D&C 121: 1
[62] 1 Nephi 16:18

happen?" Families are divided by the evil choices of parents and innocent children pay the consequences.

Recently, I had an interview with a good sister who was married to a non-member. He was a Viet Nam veteran, a foot soldier who witnessed the horrors of combat, death, and pain and walked among the most egregious horrors that can be committed by mankind. As a result of that experience, he claims to have no belief in a God of any kind. Certainly it would be difficult to build a testimony of a loving and caring God under such circumstances and easy to ask the question, "Where is God?"

I have a close friend who was dropped far beyond enemy lines with a squad of special operatives during that Viet Nam conflict. As things went terribly wrong, he found himself as a sole survivor lying wounded on the battle field and unable to move for three days. Night and day, he would stare at the passing sky in pain, contemplating his own death. Surely in these circumstances he must have asked himself, "Where is God?" His family was notified that their son was killed in action and a memorial service was held in his honor. Could his mother, under these circumstances, also ask the question, "Where was God?"

I know of a sister who was born into a member family and raised in the church. It was a well-respected family but the father was living a double life. At church they were well liked and respected. The parents held responsible callings and preformed them faithfully. However, when they went through the doors of their home, things changed. The daughter, later in life tells gruesome

172

stories of abuse. As a result, lives were destroyed, families were divided and testimonies were lost. Although totally inactive now she has a beautiful family of her own who is being raised in a good home but without the restored gospel of Jesus Christ. Certainly, in her life, she must have asked the question many times, "Where is God?"

Many faithful sisters ask themselves this question when they are facing circumstances beyond their control when an eternal companion breaks his temple covenants with unfaithful relationships. The innocent and faithful sisters recount how they *did everything right*, married in the temple, followed the prophets and honorably respected their covenants. Others find themselves pawns in the domestic disputes of the parents they love...and the list goes on.

In this struggle we call life, it is important to keep things in perspective. Heavenly Father does not create the political, social or ideological conflict that inflicts war and destruction on man, man does. Heavenly Father does not condone the abuse of children or the destruction of families, man does. Heavenly Father does not favor pain and suffering in any way for his sons and daughters no more that we would impose such things on our own children. However, they exist in the world as a result of the choices on man.

At some point in our gospel studies, we learned the plan of salvation and its origin in the "council in heaven." In order for us to become as our father, we had to come to earth, gain a body and experience the differences of good and evil. Heavenly Father understood this was a necessity in our eternal progression. He did not look forward to the difficulties it would cause us but knew it was the only way.

Even after the earth was created, he commanded Adam,

> *"And I the Lord God, commanded the man saying of every tree of the garden thou mayest freely eat, but of the tree of the knowledge of good and evil, thou salt not eat of it, nevertheless thou mayest choose for thyself for it is given unto thee: but remember that I forbid it, for in the day thou eatest thereof thou shalt surely die."[63]*

Man fell from the presence of God. It was not God's choice; He commanded against it. However, Eve partook of the fruit because she understood that, *there was no other way!*

From that day until this, the great plan of mortality has been in motion. We are a product of the choices of ourselves and those around us. We knew that there would be death and suffering before we came here and we all agreed to it. We are judged on the choices we make whether we determined our own circumstances or not. Every decision we make, is a manifestation of who we are and what we are made of. *"When the morning stars sang together, and all the sons of God shouted for joy."[64]*

---

[63] Moses 3: 16-17
[64] Job 38:7

Understanding this principle makes it easier to ask this fundamental question with some certainty. God is allowing the work to go forward *"as was counseled in the beginning to see if we will do all things whatsoever the Lord their God shall command them."*[65] He is not and will not intervene outside His divine purposes so that we can receive the full benefit of the mortal choices we make.

There is in fact, no place on land, sea or sky where God cannot be found. He is the architect and creator of all that we know and see: our bodies, our hearts and minds. He is in the wind, the air, the sunshine on our face, the cold of the winter wind and the heat of the desert sun. Our God whispers in our ear, "I am here" in the twinkle of every star of the heavens and in the song of every bird. Christ has literally "felt our pain." He cries when we cry and rejoices when we rejoice in righteousness. The plan is in motion. The earth is spinning on its predetermined axis as planned in the beginning; the "work goes forward."

To strengthen the Savior in the garden of Gethsemane Heavenly Father sent angels. To strengthen us in times of need, He sends His servants: friends, loved ones or associates for advice, comfort or council. Jesus Christ, the only begotten Son of the Father, a perfect soul who lived without sin, suffered all of the hunger, thirst, loneliness, betrayals and pain of sin of all mankind who ever lived on the earth. He was mocked, scorned, spat upon and tortured. He deserved none of this suffering. However, even in the last minutes of the live of the Lord

---

[65] Abraham 3:25

himself, the great and Eternal Father in Heaven and earth, turned away for a moment so that His perfect son could complete the work of the atonement.

Knowing His work on earth was complete, he said, *"It is finished: and he bowed his head, and gave up the ghost. "*[66] In that fleeting and passing moment Christ himself, the greatest of all at the culmination of His pain asked, *"Father, why has thou forsaken me? "*[67] But in His heart, He knew (as do we) that our Father in Heaven will never forsake us. He will never turn away. He will always be there to give us love, comfort, council and direction so long as we seek His guidance and are worth to receive it.

It may not be in the manner that we expect, but He is always there. He is a God of love, hope and charity that will forever be there and without exception, interruption or intermission. By that knowledge, we can take comfort in the fact that even in the mishaps of our lives, God is there! We just need to look beyond the chaos and see His hand in all that we are, see and feel. As we come to know and understand these principles, we will always know the answer to the question, "Where is God?"

---

[66] John 19:30
[67] Matt 27:46

Truth, Common, #: 22
Heavenly Father is cognizant
in our everyday lives.

MIRACLES HAPPEN

We were two days in on a five day hike when we approached Sassafras Mountain near the southern end of the Appalachian Trail in the mountains of Northeast Georgia. My friend Steven said that he would take the "drag" position at the rear of the "envelope" to watch over one of the slower scouts.

Shortly after arriving Sassafras Gap at the base of the mountain for lunch, I received a transmission on the FRS (Family Radio Service or "Walkie Talkie") Radio. "Andy," "Go ahead," I replied. "Steve is in trouble and needs help descending from the mountain." It would appear that a wrong step in just the wrong place forced his knee to take a position not designed for the human anatomy.

"Put him on com," I requested. As I asked Steve about his condition he simply said, "I'm done!" I knew by the tone of his voice that the injury was serious and he would not have made such a proclamation without a full understanding of the implications.

There were still ten miles of trail ahead of us before we reached our designated location for the night and another thirty miles before the hike was finished. Mixing in my concern for my friend with the complications that an emergency extraction would present, I thought, "This is going to throw a wrench in the gears." I placed my pack against a rock and walked a bit to consider the options as two other members of our party were dispatched up the trail to render assistance. It would take a while for them to bring him down with his gear.

Injuries can be painful under any circumstance, especially when you are hundreds of miles away from home and toting a fifty pound pack on your back. Common to sports, an ACL can be injured when your knee is straight and then changed directions rapidly when footing alters on shifting rocks. The abnormal bone movement can damage cartilage that covers the ends of the bones and can tear the menisci that cushion knee joints. To prolong the motion on this joint under this condition (if even possible through the pain) could break the joint; this is not a viable option in a non-life threatening situation; extraction was then the only viable option.

We try to plan for most contingencies on our hikes. Luckily, emergency trail extractions are not one of them; they are very uncommon. When things like this do happen, all of our attention changes as we focus on the problem at hand. As I ventured from the small clearing in the trees, I noticed a topographical feature known as a saddle. It is an indention in the mountain skyline where the drop from the adjoining mountain peaks meat in a changing posture from *down to up*. If there was going to be a forest road to be found in the area, they would usually find such a feature to traverse the mountainous terrain.

As I ventured a few more feet, I saw the sign identifying our location. It simply read, "Sassafras Gap" on Forest Service road #42. "Good," I thought, "at least we are close to a road." Pulling out the emergency cell phone, I quickly confirmed my suspicion that there would be no service at this remote location. If this good brother was to get off this mountain today, we would have to hike down this road until we located some assistance. It could take hours or days to accomplish the mission, but it had to be done. With nothing more to fear than a severe diversion from the planned journey, I was thankful that we were in a good location and had ample supplies to do what we needed to do.

I then returned to the group where they were just bringing our injured hiker in from the trail in a "fireman's carry." Steven sat on the ground, leaned against a large rock and groaned in pain. I could tell that he was indeed, *done*! Leaving him to face his plight, I summoned the boys and one remaining adult leader to the other end of the gap for a discussion on our options. Immediately, we considered prayer as the first order of business. With hats removed, we asked our Heavenly Father to be mindful of our friends' situation and to direct us in what we should do. Again, I walked to the forest service road and engaged the cell phone with no change in results.

At that moment, I looked down the road which revealed a four door sedan on the steep gravel grade. With two county law enforcement officers on board, I raised their attention by waving my arms. After a brief explanation of our situation, the kind officers agreed to deliver our friend Steve to the closest town where arrangements had been made (via police radio) for his wife to pick him up for a ride home. As we were loading our friend in the rear of the squad car, the officer explained, "You know, I have been in the department for over ten years and have wondered what was up this road many times but never felt inclined to come up here while on duty. But, today was so beautiful and it was so generally quite on the radio, I thought I would give it a try, and now, I am glad I did."

The officer drove down the hill with the simple impression that he had participated in an interesting coincidence that day. As we all stood there watching the illuminated brake lights pushing the cruiser down the hill, we had a real and significant knowledge that something had just happened of much greater importance. The place was no longer called Sassafras Gap; for those of us that witnessed what had just happened, it was, "Miracle Gap."

Our Heavenly Father had just issued us a personal invitation to reconsider His vigil "over watch" position in our lives. I had always believed that He was there and watching, that He would be responsive to us in prayer and

180

deed but my understanding had suddenly changed...
dramatically.

There are times when He directly intervenes in seemingly insignificant ways. The extraction of my friend Steve went so smoothly and un-dramatically that not only did the event not cause a serious disruption to our plans, it did not event take any more time that it would have to stop for lunch. We were then quickly on our way for another day on the trail while Steven was on his way home and towards medical attention.

A "tender mercy" had just been experienced, planted directly in our lives. It enriched our understanding and our testimony that our God is one of love and mercy in ways that we may never be able to understand in mortality.

It was much later in life that I came to understand how the Lord works in our lives. I grew to believe that once the earth was set on its rotating path around the sun in this universe, the Lord said, "There it is. Have fun and good luck." His interventions were transparent to my undiscerning eye. The regular every day routine became so monotonous. The spirit played an important role in my life but nothing seemed out of the ordinary. After a while, a pattern seemed to emerge. At first it was too subtle to notice but over time it became quite obvious and impossible to ignore.

It was quite often that I heard the tales from friends, family and coworkers of personal calamities occurring on a regular basis. The cars were always breaking down in the most inhospitable places leaving them dangerously stranded; there always seemed to be some terrible accident

181

somewhere affecting someone close to them or their families where always in trouble somewhere doing something. At first, I attributed my good fortune to luck but later realized that to continue that attitude was to ignore the blessings I was receiving at the Lord's hand and would deny His influence in our lives.

It actually became so frequent and obvious that I would break out in an open chuckle, look up to the Heavens and give immediate thanks for yet another tender mercy at His hand. The cars would break down, all the same, but would do so in front of a friend's house eager to lend a helping hand or near an awaiting (and convenient) parking lot where I could wait until help arrived or that time that the vehicle broke its axle just in front of a garage who just happened to be on duty and ready to fix the problem.

I was afraid to get to the point where I expected this level of personal divine attention so as not to become spoiled but I never failed to thank Him for his help. He wants to help us; He wants us to be safe and happy; we just need to stay obedient to His commandments in every way so He is free to bless us when we need it.

In studying the lives of Lamen and Lemuel, the Lord gave them every opportunity to repent and draw close to Him. He sent the spirit, messengers, righteous brothers and eventually angels but in the end, their continual disobedience led to His eventual action, total withdrawal. In the absence of His presence come the buffetings of Satan and blindness in a jungle filled with predators of every kind. It is difficult to survive such conditions. This condition fosters the decline that comes from pride and rebellion. This leads to wickedness and misery and when these principles rule, there is neither peace nor joy.

The rules of life are actually very simple, be good and be happy. Pres. Hinkley said it best when he said, "be wise and be happy or be stupid and be miserable."[68] There have always been those who believe they can make their own rules or that the rules do not apply to them. I have seen this attitude many times in my years in the Lords service but the outcome is always the same. The source of the attitude is pride which is the most common and dangerous social disorder known to men, with the church members being no exception. We must recognize this evil influence in our lives and strive to purge it from our system. "We are tempted daily to elevate ourselves above others and diminish them."[69]

If there are good among us, God will know. It is not our place, right or responsibility to determine this outside the calling of the common judge of Israel. All that is important is that we know that our Heavenly Father loves us and will affect our lives on a regular basis if we remain worthy of His blessings. The pursuit of this goal will bring blessings, happiness and joy. Everything else, will take care of itself.

---

[68] Grodon B. Hinkley 2007
[69] Beware of Pride, Ezra Taft Benson

A MESSAGE FROM THE DUST
... OF LIFE

Though we have been counseled to keep a journal, I have had a hard time complying. In an effort to remain obedient in all things, I purchased a prepackaged "journal" from a church book store; it is still only three quarters full after forty years of life's experiences. The explanation seems simple; I don't want to remember the events of my life. For the most part, I perceived them to be painful and would choose to have them forgotten rather than remembered.

In some cases, I remember tearing the pages from the hard cover binding after the events were memorialized rather than considering the possibility of ever having to recognize the reality of the events that had taken place. I am sure that my life is no harder than most others and would surely be embarrassed at point-to-point comparison but pain is pain no matter how or who administers it.

These difficult life experiences drove me to high risk activities which brought me to the edge of death many times. Looking back now, I can see that this eventuality was an acceptable conclusion but through them all, I remain. I have often asked myself "why" I have been sustained here on earth after obviously deserving or even choosing to end the daily ritual of stress, turmoil and inner conflict. Through the years of accumulated life's experiences and the wisdom that accompanies them I can only come to conclude that there must be someone out there that can benefit from these words.

I have heard it said, "No one is totally worthless, they can always be used as a good bad example!" Surely this applies to me. Therefore in an effort to fulfill the Lords purpose for the revelry of my life, I will attempt to look back and review some experiences and subsequent messages I would have for the world just in case He loses His will to keep me here the next time I present Him the choice.

At first glance, it would appear that the lessons I would share with you are a tangled narrative of "random streams of consciousness" as my wife would say. I have been called an awful writer for this very reason. As the efforts of others to sanitize my style have become frustrated, I offer these lessons *from the heart* to the willing heart to hear the intent and the spirit that the message contain rather than the unwashed style in which it is presented.

The things I have come to know are true came *the hard way.* There were usually no one there testifying of its truthfulness, or celebrated text book pointing out the facts in logical detail. They were learned by rigid and mostly painful methods. These are the lessons that are not soon forgotten, if ever. With implants of truth etched in the stone of my mind, I have become hard and rigid in resolve and opinion. This is offensive to many and something I have had to deal with many times in my life, mostly in connection with the opportunities the Lord has given me to counsel with His sons and daughters of His Church. The Lord has been very kind to me in this regard but has always dealt with me harshly, or so I perceived.

I was in my early forties when I finally sought professional help for my inability to recognize the value for my life. This good and spiritual counselor asked me, "Does the Lord answer your prayers?" "Yes," I replied, "but the answers always come in sideways." "What do you mean," he questioned. "Well, I get the answers but He always follows up or precedes the answer with, sarcasm or even with an affront that I would have asked such a foolish question in the first place."

It was in wisdom and insight that he leaned back in his chair and with a gentle smile on his face asked me the question, "Tell me about your father." It only took a moment for me to understand where he was going in this line of questioning. My concept of father was formed at an early age. My dad was a harsh disciplinarian who never forsook the responsibility of utilizing the *rod* so as to not *spoil the child.*

I remember as a child playing in the trees behind the church building one Sunday afternoon while my parents were in a meeting, or so I thought. Being about ten years old and not having a concept of the passing of time while climbing the magnificent southern magnolia trees that filled the parking lot with shade, I was found by my dad with the proclamation that I made him look for me two hours and he was greatly delayed from his routine. I was told that I would be taught a lesson when we got home. This became a reality. For me, that afternoon hosted a brutal reprisal at the hands of a father that would scar our relationship for the rest or our lives. The punishment hardly "met the crime."

My childhood and professional life were filled with *whippings* that seemed to follow in endless succession. Through it all, I learned to love my wife and children as a spiteful accolade to the bitterness I was taught as a child. My kids were raised in a way that I wish I had been raised. They all grew to be wonderful successful, good and righteous people who love the Lord. Of course, most of this success, I attribute to my faithful companion who shares my desire to raise them in the Gospel of Jesus Christ and to show them the "iron rod"[70] of life.

It was a constant and regular prayer that I offered to the Lord with the fullness of heart and faith that I desired the "purpose for my life" and its difficult circumstances. It was forty years later that the answer was finally received. It is at these moments that we look back with curious perspective to put our lives in order. It is in these moments

---

[70] The word of God: 1 Nephi 11:25

that we see that the Lord is *curious* in His ways and that they are *not our ways.*[71]

Our lives seem to be filled with dust that is stirred up in our daily activity. By sheer velocity of speed and impact on the dirt track of the earth, dust fills the air to where it often becomes difficult to see anything behind or in front of us much less off in the distance. It takes time for the dust to settle. This cannot happen until we stop and allow this to happen. Stopping is often not possible unit our hearts and lungs are quiet and motionless.

However, there is wisdom coming from beyond the dust of life, from those who have gone before and from those who have traveled the same road. They stand at the wayside to offer gentle counsel. They have traveled the road and have returned to the most difficult turns, narrow bridges and side cliffs to lend a hand and offer advice. Feeling lucky to have survived its hazards, they return as if to fulfill an obligation to the fates that successfully delivered them safely to the end.

I humbly submit myself as one of these messengers. I see that it is only through the will of God that I survived the road (so far). I now return by obligation to Him that saw me through to offer whatever helpful advice I can to aid you in your pursuit of truth.

My messages are the ones that the Lord gave to me. You may take them as proprietary to my individual circumstance or pray to see how you may benefit from the "bad example" I may have been in the lives of some.

---

[71]Isaiah 55:8

Hopefully, it will not be many. I only speak the truth as I have come to know it. I am not politically correct by purpose and design. I do not have time, desire or inclination for it as message is often lost or diluted in a swirl of "fluff." It will be up to you to see how the lessons I learned in my life applies to you.

Hopefully, you will learn the lessons of life in a much more pleasant manner than me. In either case, I am thankful for the lessons I wished I never had. These are all simple messages...messages from the dust.

Truth, Common #:24
    Everything has its purpose

UNDERSTANDING THE "WHY"

In the short time I have been on this earth (relatively speaking) I continue to ask the question, "why?" Why does it have to be this way? Why does it have to be so hard? Can't the pressure let up for just a little bit?

As a spiritual counselor, I have been asked many times by those seeking these answers to tell them what they should do. "Just tell me," they plead. To my memory, I have never succumbed to this request. We simply go through the situation together and begin the attempt to understand "why" they must figure it out for themselves. Mostly because the situation is uniquely theirs and no one is qualified to answer for themselves better than they are. Otherwise, it would give them no "ownership" and hold no lasting conviction in their heart that the answer was what the Lord intended. Our Heavenly Father leads us along, line upon line, precept upon precept, here a little, there a little. It seems easy to understand but to abide by this truth becomes harder as the phases of life separate so severely.

When I was a youngster, I wondered why it was so hard to be small. When would I be able to take care of myself? As I entered young adult hood the questions concentrated around the future and when I would be self-supportive. As a young father, I wondered how I would ever endure the relentless and endless responsibility surrounding the children.

The kids are all gone now and the home is quiet. I sit at my keyboard in the bedroom converted office once hosting three boys is close succession. They have families of their own now as do their sisters who are following in succession of life's phases as I did and my parents before me. Looking back, it does not seem so long now, as the years I thought would never end, have passed as a summer breeze through the pines.

I feel as though I have "completed my mission" and the debriefing has been completed. I have been extremely blessed to have served a life time in the kingdom of God on earth and have loved it. So, at what point do we declare, "Game Over?" The simple answer is, "never!"

Though I have developed a certain level of understanding in the matters I have had experience, it is insignificant in the matters that are yet to be explored and understood. We cannot build on one precept until we understand it, then we can move on. It is not enough to

191

survive or endure our trials, we must learn from them, understand them. Otherwise, the same trials will continue until we learn to avoid them or deal with them so precisely that they are no longer trials; they are simply matters to dispatch. It is the "understanding" part that so many of us have a problem with.

I remember many times kneeling at the side of my bed at the end of a particular gruesome day saying, "Heavenly Father, I am thankful for this day" and feeling really stupid. I was not thankful for that day but figured it must have been "for my own good" in some sort of twisted way. As a result, I would follow up with, "please help me to understand why this day was necessary?" I don't know that I ever received an immediate response but somewhere along the way, the answers would come.

It is the *understanding* that keeps us from going crazy.

- I understand that the only way that vegetables will grow in my garden is to work to keep the choking grass away. I don't like doing it but understand it is necessary.
- I hate putting gas in my car because the price is ridiculous and I never have the time. However, if I don't, I understand that the car will not function.
- I do not enjoy having to take the trash to the street but understand that if I don't it will pile up and create a bigger problem.

Likewise, issues in our lives are similar.

- Providing discipline for our children is difficult but if we don't, they will have no structure and may live an "undisciplined life." This is understandable.
- Living the "word of wisdom" is difficult and inconvenient at times but if we don't, we submit ourselves to all of the hazards associated with the use of harmful substances in our bodies. This is understandable.
- Obeying the commandments will certainly limit our leisure activities. However, I understand that if I do this, I am promised eternal life.

Understanding the "why" behind the "do" is essential to our calm temperament. The *why* may be as simple as, *"I know not save the Lord commanded me."*[72] The *understanding* involved in this case is that we know that we love the Lord. The Lord has asked us to do it so we do. It is as simple as that. In many cases that is enough. In other cases it is important to understand the why behind the commandment.

In every case however, we need to understand who we are and what we are doing here. We need to understand why we are doing what we are doing and where it is taking us. Once these concepts become more clear, we can begin to be of greatest benefit to our Father in Heaven as He uses us as instruments in His hands to help others in their "Pursuit of Understanding." After all, that is what life is, right?

---

[72] Moses 5:6

Common, Truth #: 25

It is important that we learn <u>who</u> we should listen to.

STAY ALERT, STAY ALIVE

It was early in my military training that I heard the phrase, "Stay alert, stay alive." When we heard this phrase it was usually quickly followed by some command of *drill and ceremony* (D&C) that needed immediate and skillful execution. It was a warning to watch out for the following instruction but later became an icon for the environment we were to enter.

Likewise, this phrase can become useful in our lives every day. *"For behold, at that day he shall rage in the hearts of the children of men...All is well in Zion; yea Zion prospereth."*[73] This scripture warns of the day that wickedness will reign in the hearts of man but there will be

---

[73] 2 Nephi 28:20-21

those that are *at ease in Zion.*[74] The Lord is telling us to "watch out" for danger.

At several places in the Book of Mormon, we learn of towers that were built for the watchmen. On one occasion, the wicked king Noah climbed the tower fleeing from Gideon when he saw the approaching Lamanite army and pled for his life. It was not until Noah climbed the tower did he notice the danger approaching. It is therefore critical that each of us have an "over watch position" in our lives; this however, usually creates a problem. The top of the tower is usually cold and lonely.   The lookouts cannot stay there as they have lives on the surface.

The Lord has provided a way for us to have the benefit of an early warning system without having to live atop the tower. *"And set a watchmen round about them and build a tower, that one may overlook the land round about...that my olive trees may not be broken down by my enemies...when they come to spoil."*[75]

It would appear that this scripture is literal and figurative at the same time. There are many "towers" in our lives. If we consider the fact that a tower is any object that allows you to see beyond your current position or prospective, a tower can be parents, leaders, scriptures and the temple itself.

Watchmen are those who can see far off. It is those appointed by the Lord to watch and warn His children.

---

[74] V 24
[75] D&C 101:45

They should include Bishops, Stake Presidents and the Prophets of our day.

When the watchman warns of an impending threat, we exercise our plan to meet and overcome it. If we are prepared, we will not fear.[76] If we are not prepared, fear sets in. In one context," fear is spoken of as something unworthy of a child of God, something that "perfect love casteth out."[77] We learn from the teachings of John that, *"There is no fear in love; but perfect love casteth out fear: because fear hath torment. He that feareth is not made perfect in love."*[78] As the Lords love for us is perfect, He wants us to fear not.

I have often thought that the point was missed completely when I have heard many in the church to rehearse the verse, "If ye are prepared, ye shall not fear" almost as an excuse to discredit those who profess preparation. Preparation can be interpreted in many different ways. Often, it is interpreted to just "not fear" without the preparation component attached. In this admonition not to fear, the Lord did not imply that there would not be calamities; He said to be prepared and in this effort it is always good to know what we need to prepare for.

Here are some examples:

- We may fear those people who can hurt us.

---

[76] Gordon B. Hinkley 2005
[77] Bible Dictionary
[78] 1 John 4:18

- We fear the cold if we know that we cannot become warm.
- We may fear the dark if we do not know what threat it hides.
- We fear the forest because of the unknown predators which lurk there.
- We fear attacks to our weakest fortifications.

If we have no weaknesses, we will have no fear. This however, is an impossible contingency. Each of us has weaknesses, some more than others, but have them we do. We must identify and strengthen each of our weaknesses one at a time and plug the largest breach in our outer wall of defense first.

Being delivered from the throne of God to earth in innocence, we enter a world filled with infinite agendas. We may or may not be welcome to those instrumental to to those who placed the order for the development of our earthly tabernacle, but life comes to us all the same. As hatchling turtles left on the beach of life to fend for ourselves, many scramble to the protection of the awaiting seas for survival while most perish under the awaiting beaks of sailing predators eager to terminate our advance for personal gratification.

Only to be momentarily satisfied by the carnivorous consumption, they patiently but anxiously await the next round of hatchlings.

This scene of destruction grieves the parents but there is only so much they can do to protect us. Either at infancy or in adulthood, the young will eventually have to face those that would destroy them. This destruction can come in many forms. The predators may come disguised as friends who carefully lead the destroyer directly to the door to feed at his pleasure. Learning to recognize the difference between "friend or foe" can be one of the most difficult challenges of life if it were not for the guidance of the Holy Ghost.

This third member of the Godhead occupies the tallest tower on earth as its unlimited vision provides unrestricted information on our path and the road in front of us. With the certainty of predators in our lives, it is critical that we choose a *watchman on the tower* that will never sleep, never tire and never fail to call the alert when needed.

Know that there is no earthly watchman capable of providing the direction of this holy messenger of the Father. With the direction and guidance from Him, there will always be the drumming of words mixed in the cadence of life warning us to "stay alert, and stay alive."

SECTION 4

"Acquired truth"

Service
in
the Kingdom

"We learn as we serve."

Our understanding increases as we become instruments in
the Lord's hand to do His will in the lives of His children.
Through this service and sacrifice, we see them as He sees
them and increases our understanding beyond anything
otherwise possible.

Acquired, truth #: 26
There is wisdom in the use of the lay ministry in the
Kingdom of God on earth.

A FEW GOOD MEN

It is often the case that when someone decides to become less active in the Church, they site something someone did at one point or another. They say that those who called them (the offending leader) should have known better because **they** were "called and set apart" through inspiration. This inspiration could not have come from Heavenly Father because the person had so many shortcomings, the calling could not have inspired, therefore the whole structure of their testimony collapses over the one brick pulled from its foundation. It seems like such sound logic in the mind where understanding is lacking. It fits well in the category of excuses permitting relief from the disciplined life style taught by the church.

There have in fact, been many leaders in the church that fit into this category in my lifetime. I am sure that many have felt the same way about me and have taken offense to something I have said or done.

President Gordon B. Hinckley once told a group of assembled missionaries, "You are not much to look at but you are all the Lord has."[79] When I think of his good natured humor and quick wit comment, I believe this adage can be applied to most, if not all, (at least among the brethren) of those who are called to serve.

It is not yet time for Christ to rule on the earth. He is not physically here to dispel the evil words and deeds of man. He has used the power of the Holy Ghost to inspire His children to come to him and follow in His footsteps. Though, Christ himself was, *"no form nor comeliness and when we shall see him there is no beauty that we should desire him."*[80] He was the creator of the earth and man. It was the inner man, the heart and spirit that determined who He was. He knows that this same principle applies to us.

The Church of Jesus Christ of Latter Day Saints is operated by lay ministry; there is no paid clergy. As Peter was taken from the deck of the fishing boat and asked to *"follow me and I will make you fishers of man,"*[81] the same technique is used today. Men do not call themselves to the ministry; they are called of God through inspiration as described in the fifth Article of Faith "We believe that a man must be called of God by prophecy and by the laying

---

[79] Grodon B. Hinkley, Gen Priesthood address
[80] Isaiah 53:2
[81] Matt 4:19

on of hands by those who are in authority to preach the Gospel and administer in the ordinances thereof."

Often, mistakes are made by good men who want to do the right thing but are caught up in difficult circumstances that have many possible outcomes, with some being better than others. We may find ourselves on the end of that decision that maybe did not turn out so good. Is this a reason to declare with singularity that the boy prophet Joseph Smith did not receive a vision? As absurd as this leap of logic may seem, it is exactly what happens in many cases. Because there is one insignificant leak in the dam of judgment, the lake is drained for failure to contain its contents.

At every level from Priesthood and Auxiliary, saints from all walks of life and from every background, accept the call to serve. It is hard to understand the infinite personal and professional backgrounds held by the leaders of the Church. They bring with them all that they are and all that they have learned to the responsibilities they are given. It is this diversity that brings strength to the work. It is also however, what brings strong wills, dispositions and personalities. Herein lies the challenge of people working with people.

In most cases, the mistakes that are made are misjudgments with little consequence outside some hurt feelings with the specific individuals involved. However, in rare and exceptional cases, decisions are made by those in positions of significant responsibility that bring grave concern.

I was once privileged to be among the brethren who knelt in humble prayer asking for direction in the calling of a new leader in a branch. Collectively, and individually, our thoughts and minds were calm as we recommended the name of a brother to fill the position of Branch President. The confirming spirit was received and we issued the calling. As time progressed, a serious moral infraction was exposed revealing to this brother's conduct outlining abuse justifying incarceration for the remainder of his life. Legal action was taken and justice was served. All that remained was the shattered emotional lives of the victims and the questions of how such a thing could happen; how could this man had been called by God knowing what he was?

When the Old Testament prophet Samuel was directed by the Lord to call Saul to be king over Judea, did the Lord know what kind of person Saul was and what he was capable of? Well of course He did. So, why was the calling made? Why would the Lord call a man to be king knowing that he would later abuse his power, corrupt the kingdom and seek to murder David?

There are of course, many explanations of which we could delineate one by one. Each of these explanations would be perfectly logical and explain the divine nature of our Father in Heaven. However, all that we really need to understand is that the Lord is peculiar in His ways.[82]

The thing that I have come to understand is that there are times when the Lord called the very best person for the job by virtue of their spirit, skill set and willingness

---

[82] Elder Clayton M. Christensen, 2007, My Ways are not Your Ways

to serve. They are a blessing to all that serve with them and great things are accomplished.

In other cases, He calls those who are a test to those they serve. It is a test of their faith, their will and ability to be loyal to the kingdom in spite of opposition placed **directly** in their spiritual path.

We know of many cases in the scriptures where the Lord has used this technique. Alma rose from the spiritual oppression of the wicked king Noah to become one of the most faithful and inspiring leaders of the church. As mentioned, David rose to be king of Judea after escaping near death by the hand of the man called of God to lead him.

The Prophet Mormon refused the leadership of the armies due to the wickedness of the people but later accepted the calling because of his love for them. It is often through these types of environments that great leaders emerge with a greater understanding of how things should and should not be done. Is there an environment more conducive to learning than one where you experience its effects first hand?

It is in the pressure cooker where meals are prepared to become most palatable to the appetite. Steam is forced into the tough cavities of the food and it is softened becoming most yummy! Why are we any different? Sometimes, it takes the pressure cooker of life to bring us to our knees to ask our Heavenly Father why; how could such a thing be allowed to happen? In the process of receiving the answerer to this prayer (which is offered in prayer and fasting) that we receive many precious answers pertaining to many aspects of our life.

Similarly, the Prophet Joseph asked this question after being falsely accused and left to squander in the dungeon of Liberty Jail. A righteous man in the clutches of wicked men with evil purposes, he had all the reasons in the world to ask the Lord this hard question. The answer from the Lord has served to be one of the most precious and rehearsed revelation used in the church.... *"know thou, my son, that all these things shall give thee experience, and shall be for thy good."*[83]

The physical world is not a place of justice. Proof of this screamed from every news cast, paper and transmission available to mankind today. Governments, societies and entire cultures suppress liberties, freedoms, choices and movements that oppose their rule. Religion cannot even be mentioned in many countries much less taught.

As mentioned in the Doctrine and Covenants, we are here to gain experience, not justice and in many sad cases, it happens within the sacred walls of our own *house.* One thing is certain however, this injustice in the Kingdom of God will not be tolerated, for *"the house of god is a house of order."*[84]

We can all take great comfort in the fact that we are led by a choice Prophet of God who would never be allowed to lead us astray.[85] To the extent he can share his

---

[83] D&C 122:7
[84] ibid
[85] Liahona June 1981, Fourteen Fundamentals in Following the Prophet

love, counsel and guidance, such tragedies in leadership will never be intentionally allowed. All of us follow the spirit as it directs us in this holy work. We are constantly in their thoughts and prayers.

We will be judged on our own hearts and minds and our willingness to serve the Lord. He knows all things, including the hearts and minds of those giving us leadership. We will be held accountable for our obedience to Him, our leaders will be held accountable for the same as well as their council to us.

It is important that we remain focused on our own salvation and let the Lord and His chosen leaders to deal justly with those called to serve us, even though they may not be much to look at! All He needs is a few good men.

The Lord uses the right tool for the right job at the right time.

THE MANY TOOLS OF THE CARPENTER

(Which one are you?)

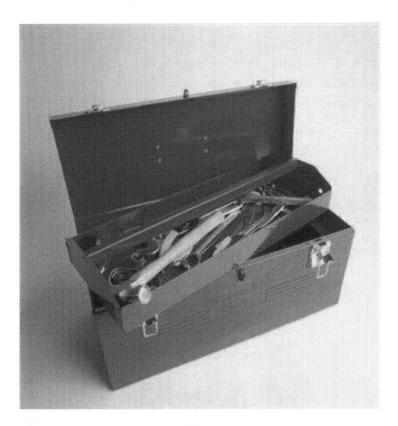

With activity in the Church of Jesus Christ of Latter Day Saints come one particular certain eventuality: callings. President Hinckley once recited a poem that has become among my favorite, "Mary had a little lamb. It grew into a sheep. Then it joined the Mormon Church and died for lack of sleep."[86] Callings can be the greatest and the most stressful events in our lives all at the same time.

It is through wisdom that the Lord gives us responsibilities to exercise our faith and stretch our abilities. It has been my privilege in life to be raised in the country where it is essential to maintain land, lambs and lentils. There was always grass to cut, animals to feed and gardens to maintain. Being the only son of five kids, the "outside" responsibility seemed to be mine.

For each of these responsibilities, there was a tool. As a result, I grew to love and appreciate tools. Some of the tools were specific to the specific job but in other cases they had multiple uses. For example, a hammer could be used for many things from driving a nail to getting attention of the family mule. Also, I found it quite effective for making *fine* adjustments to radios and televisions. Pliers are also awesome tools; they pinch stuff! They can be used for holding something in place or forcing a stubborn bolt into submission. They can also be used for removing a thorn from your finger. Pliers, hammers and screwdrivers are multipurpose tools but still come in a variety of sizes.

Specialty tools include wrenches, sockets, taps and

---

86 Gordon B. Hinkley (personal knowledge)

dies, saws and drills. Each are made for a specific size and application. They are intended for one job only. As a result, they do the job better than any multipurpose tool can. However, use outside of its intended application is limited. In order to be effective on any sizeable job, you need to have many such tools, each designed for a purpose and it must be sturdy enough to endure the anticipated pressures without breaking.

Sockets intended for the impact wrench are specially made for the increased stress but are larger and bulkier as a result. The small shinny ones are quick, fast and easy but more fragile and more likely to break under maximum stress. To be effective, you need to know the approximate torque requirements before selecting the appropriate socket. Likewise, wrenches come in all sizes. They are metric and standard, box and open, six and twelve point. There are some that are Torx bit, some Allen head, some Spline and some swivel each to its own application. In many cases, only one will do. The job simply will not accept any other tool; it can only be manipulated with the one that fits, that's all.

If you try to improvise and use a tool for the job that will not fit, it will cause complications or even damage the project you are working on. A skilled craftsman knows the job, the tools needed and how to use the tools to do the job.

After experiencing a number of jobs with varying needs, the craftsman realizes that there are many different tools he needs to assemble so they will be ready when the need arises. Many of them will stand ready but not be called on because a bolt or nut representing their size application was not encountered. On the next job however, the needs will be different and the tools used will vary.

There are some tools that are used in nearly every job for various reasons. There are other jobs that require a tool that may be rarely used. It usually stays in the bottom of the tool cabinet but when it is needed, nothing else will suffice. It will collect dust until the need arises when it is pulled out, cleaned up and applied to the full measure of its creation. It is then returned to its appointed place as we draw joy in the benefit of its special services.

To study the various jobs and needs in the service, manufacturing, industrial and business realms it is easy to imagine the need for an infinite number of tools. In the hands of the trained and skilled craftsman, they can accomplish amazing tasks. In the hands of the uninformed and unskilled, they are simply strange objects that defy imagination.

As we consider each of these tools, is it fair to ask the question, "Which is better?" Discounting the discussion of quality, does this remain a valid question? Is a ½" wrench better than a ¾" wrench? Is a shovel better than a rake, a hammer better than a punch or a tractor better than a car? Of course, none of these questions can be answered before we consider what the specific job (need) is.

As I think of our callings and people in the kingdom, I often think of tools and the correlation. Many times I have contemplated matching jobs and people to

211

serve the Lord. The discussion never involves "which is best" but rather "which is right?" Each job in the church has a specific application. There is a ½" nut that needs to be turned and a nail that needs to be driven in place; this is not the time to crank up the lawn mower. It is time to go to the tool box, not the garden shed. I cannot effectively maintain the residence without the lawn mower; it is just not what is needed at this time.

The wards and branches of the Church are usually filled with talented saints who are willing and anxious to serve. The Lord gives "Keys" to the leaders to have insight into the will of God. He knows the jobs and available tools better than we do. As leaders, we listen to the promptings to understand what the job is and who the most effective tool to do the job.

In our worldly insight, we see a ½" nut that is in fact a ¾" bolt; only the Lord knows. Bishops, Branch Presidents, Quorum and Auxiliary leaders come in all sizes, shapes capacities and temperaments. In some cases, a general application tool will suffice when in other cases; specific specialized tools will only do the job. In most cases, there are several if not many that will do the job and do it well but only the Lord knows what the job will require in the future. We rely on Him to pick the right tool out of the box for the right job at the right time.

We may all be tools in the box to be used for His divine purposes. It is important for us to always be worthy to remain in the box when the time comes for us to fill the measure of our creation. It is important to understand this principle so we can become the best tool for who or what we are and understand that we are no better or worse than the tool next to us; we are just different. The carpenter uses many tools. Which one are you?

Truth, Acquired#: 28

A transition is inevitable in the life of a person who embraces the Gospel of Jesus Christ

MORMON

(It's not *what* but *who* we are!)

The building was bare, cold and dark as I turned the Medco[87] key to begin the day. With the foyer area vacant and still, I peered down the long sisal covered hallways adorning the laminated oak doors leading to the extremities of the facility. The gentle melodic hum of the mechanical airways comes to life to prepare for the Sabbath. It is quiet as I open the double folding doors leading to the chapel. The pulpit is rising above the simple stained woodwork silently welcoming my arrival.

The space devoid of movement, sound or activity, is indeed empty for those looking for a physical presence. I quietly move to the center of the back row and fill my

---

[87] Medco tm

senses with the scene. With arms folded, I lean back knowing that I was alone but deeply aware that my presence there was insignificant comparatively.

The memories of the souls of the countless inspired messengers that once filled this edifice, is ever present as is the spirit left in their wake. The growing illumination from the metal halide lights reach maturity as the elements warm in their lofty mounts. Chairs carefully placed in position by saints, align themselves *dress-right-dress* in the overflows anticipating the spiritual instruction that will be delivered this day.

As I ponder the work, the Gospel and the people and all those that call this place *home,* I realize something, something special; we are unique, perhaps peculiar. Knowing at that moment that there is no place in the world I would rather be, I wonder, what is it that makes us different? I have non-member friends that call us weird. I am afraid that I would have to agree.

It was the Prophet that declared "Let us here observe that a religion that does not require a sacrifice of all things never has power sufficient to produce the faith necessary unto life and salvation."[88] This is a unique teaching of our day and one that drives the faith of those aspiring to meet this qualification.

The history of The Church of Jesus Christ of Latter Day Saints is filled with stories of sacrifice. The road to its modern acceptance is covered with the toil, labor and the blood of its people. We take strength from stories from

---

[88] Lectures on faith pg 69

those that faced the mobs but stood fast in their conviction. Often, we question ourselves if we would have been strong enough to face the challenges and overcome the opposition.

This strength is handed down in the blood of the heritage of generations literally and figuratively. We share in the legacy of faith as we join the kingdom, grasp and embrace its principles and live its teachings.

Being a Mormon is not a label so much as it is an identity. As we join ourselves with the saints and become part of their social network it is *what* we are, but at some point through faithfulness and diligence, it becomes *who* we are.

It was in a University Branch that I saw a young sister attend her first meeting of the Mormon faith. She was approached by two inspired missionaries to hear the gospel as she was driving the university bus on its appointed route. From this unlikely approach, the young sister accepted the invitation and came willing to listen and learn.

My first impression was that this sister was *brought in from the world* as her countenance exuded cautious inquiry to the message. Over a passage of time, this sister accepted the Gospel, embraced it and became fully involved in its teachings, practices and traditions. I later witnessed a different countenance altogether. She had a glow about her. Her face was filled with light and her spirit with charity. It was the Gospel of Jesus Christ, in its fullness, that took her from *what* she was to *who* she became. In every sense of the word, she became a Mormon. It was no longer a title or a group association, it was her identity; a daughter of God who came to realize her potential and position in His eternal family. It was from that moment that I called her Sister Sunshine.

The glowing countenance is a natural consequence of conversion. Becoming a part of something you know to be true and seeing its joyful message exercised in your life. This is what and who we are, Mormons.

This strength of conviction is a source of frustration for those what would steer us astray. Many churches in our neighborhoods caution their members to avoid conversation with Mormons because the odds of turning our resolve are not worth the risk. It has become a regular occurrence for me to receive hostility immediately following the revelation of my church identity before the thought of rational dialogue is considered.

The light that changes the lives of those that become converted to the restored Gospel is the same light that they fear will expose the dim existence of their own sound doctrine. With this understanding, it is simple to understand why the members of the Church become targets of the adversary. It has always been thus,

> *"I soon found, however, that my telling the story had excited a great deal of prejudice against me among professors of religion and was the cause of great persecution, which continued to increase; and though I was an obscure boy, only between fourteen and fifteen years of age and my circumstances in life such as to make a boy of no consequence in the*

*world, yet men of high standing would take
notice sufficient to excite the public mind
against me and create a bitter persecution and
this was a common among all the sects and
united to persecute me.* "[89]

Though small and insignificant, the lad and his
message posed a grave threat to the enemy of righteousness
and all those who followed him. It is in fact, the same battle
we face today. Individually, we are small and insignificant
to the world stage but what we are threatens every modern
priest craft that fuels the engine of spiritual corruption,
confusion and desecration.

What we are may be changed in some ways.
"What," can be a title, a position or affiliation that may
change with callings, appointments or assignments. Who
we are is a representation of personal identity. It is a state
of mind, a state of being or of existence. No outside
affiliation can change that; no matter where we are, we are
always who we are.

We are members of The Church of Jesus Christ of
Latter Day Saints; we are Mormons. This is an identity that
describes our soul, our character and our moral fiber. To be
truly converted is to be rock solid in conviction and
immoveable in our desire to always follow Him, and be a
soldier in the Army of God to seek out and rescue those
imbedded in our ranks that have the sunshine in their souls
looking for the portal to display its glow. The portal is the

---

[89] JSH:22

message of the restored Gospel in its fullness and once received can never be extinguished.

The self-declaration of our identity in the *who* we are cannot be recognized by our words alone, it is by our actions. To become identified as a *who* we must be beyond the realm of spiritual reproach. This can only be proven by our continued commitment to the work in all that we do and say over the passage of our lives. In fact, it may only be in the declaration of the Savior Himself on the welcoming side of the veil where we hear the words "well done thou good and faithful servant" that we know that *who* we were holds true, a Mormon.

Truth, Acquired #: 29
         The truth can always be shielded
     when the information is controlled.

WITH A GOOD IMAGE, YOU CAN GET AWAY WITH ANYTHING

(Tiananmen Square)

It is often said that the lessons learned "hardest" (the ones most painful) are the ones learned best (not soon forgotten). It is through these collective experiences that we begin to understand certain things with greater clarity. One of the most important pearls of wisdom we acquire is the firm understanding that things are not often as they appear.

The concept of "image" and the perception of it being positive and pleasing is the subject of hours of research and the expenditures of fortunes. Entire fields of thought are devoted to this practice by professionals and self-appointed experts across the globe. Obviously this is necessary to promote a positive response to the solicitation of products, services or the quality of individuals and even governments. This effort is mandated to create an *identity* or an illusion of one.

In most cases, these carefully researched, planned and executed campaigns are successful as the oblivious masses willfully accept the pleasing rhetoric as fact. Skillfully trained apologists prepare a tasteful meal for your mental palette to taste as sweet and desirable.

The actual product however, may be quite different than what is portrayed. In most cases, it is only after consumption that you realize that the product falls short of expectation. Luckily, you made the decision and that is exactly what the advertiser is counting on; you bought it!

The application of this principle is utilized in all walks of life. As individuals, most of us are careful to create an image of ourselves. Our image is displayed in our walk, talk and personal presentation. How often is it that those you know personally are actually *genuine,* without pretense or illusion? Are they the same people on the *inside* as they are on the *outside*? Sadly, many of our friends and associates fail the test. This concept of "self" falls short of their reality necessitating an "illusion" to an identify they are otherwise unable to obtain.

There have been many among us who have been "taken in" by the image of a friend, associate or even a loved one who has turned out to be a very different person than what we were led to believe. The consequences of correcting this misguided alliance can be particularly painful.

I believe that mankind is basically good and trusting. We "want" to believe and accept those that we trust. It is in the "evolution of understanding" that we realize that we must look beyond the obvious. The following is an example.

We entered the inner city square of Beijing, China on a crisp, clear spring morning. It was a joyful time for vacationers and local residents to enjoy a day in an area that translates to mean "Gate of Heavenly Peace." Advertised to be the largest city square in the world, Tiananmen Square displays a shrine to their late and honored leader, Mao Zedong. His mammoth painted image presides over the expansive plaza.

Once this lovely square hosted thousands of young citizens seeking freedom of speech and basic liberties from the totalitarian communist regime. As the students' determination built frustration in the ruling communist class, their fate was decided at the end of a gun.

As the joyful tourists around me strolled upon the carefully prepared image of the attractive surroundings that spring day on the square, they were taking pictures and exchanging accolades of its beauty. In my mind, the spirit was screaming as it acknowledged the shattering sounds of horror as machine guns opened up on the innocence once present there. As if calling from the dust of the past, their cries of terror ripped across the summer sky to fill the air and declare to the uninformed world that a mammoth miscarriage of "image" was being propagated among them.

Though the blood had been washed away, the bodies removed and the "image" restored, the evidence embedded of the murders was not totally removed. The ancient stone blocks covering the ground refused to surrender the evidence of the 7.62x39 Warsaw pact projectiles used that fateful day of June 4, 1989 that took between 250 to 2500 lives.

As the cameras were darkened, the microphones silenced and critical eyes turned, the "People's Liberation Army" of China mowed down the bodies of their brothers and sisters, sons and daughters, as they would the nuisance blades of grass from the surface of their "garden," the shrine of totalitarianism, Tiananmen Square. Commensurate with the Kingsmen of old, domination of the subservient class must be maintained.

With the illustrious Communist Parliament Building overlooking the scene, it is easy to believe that Godless patriarch who orchestrated the "cultural revolution" would have approved. The "image" of the modern and enlightened China was intact to welcome all visitors and to promote "good will."

It is interesting that during my visit there, none of the young people I spoke with had any knowledge of the event. It would seem that the troublesome incident was erased from history. However, there was one young man in his 30's who lived in Beijing during the time and knew something had happened. As his father, living near the square, heard the sounds and surmised what had occurred, it became translated as a "necessary evil to help move the government toward reform," evidence that a positive campaign of "image" is effective once information can be controlled.

It is obvious that Satan's message is being received "very well" by much of the world as Satan's ways have been wrapped in a positive image. Good is bad and bad is good! The image is whatever you want it to be and with enough resources, can be purchased through skillful advertising. It can be strict or lenient, narrow or broad, confining or liberating.

There is a "religion" for every taste, every appetite and every hunger for knowledge. It will come in tasteful packaging pleasing to the eye and delightful to our hunger for acceptability and commensurate with those sharing our desired self "image."

Image is indeed important; we need to decide if we want it to be real or an illusion. "Ye shall know them by their fruits."[90] The beautiful outward image of that Hollywood celebrity, is often an illusion of the corrosive and corruptible spirit it frames. That handsome, dynamic and successful man in the fashionably tailored suit is often an illusion or a selfish narcissist who has little interest to meet the needs of anyone beyond himself.

Life is full of examples of which we could all fill in the blanks with names, dates and places. The most important lesson learned is the critical principal that we must always look beyond the obvious, past the *prepared image* and know that, ye shall know a prophet by its fruits. This is wisdom and a place where it is applied in our lives as increased understanding. This makes us smarter and happier.

---

[90] 3 Nephi 14:16

FINDING THE TRUTH

(In the Haystack of the modern Apostolic proclamations)

It has always been interesting to me how some religious sects claim the exclusive privilege of determining the definition of Christianity and who are allowed to be called Christian. It would appear that in an effort to lay claim to the *Christian* copyright, there would be those who unilaterally claim exclusivity to the honorable designation according to how it fits within their narrow definitions and in accordance with their personal interests.

It is in this order of self-righteousness that they deny the power of God and act as self-appointed embassaries to qualify and sanitize the masses of humanity. In itself, it could be the reason that God the Father declared

225

to a boy prophet that *"They draw close to me with their lips but their hearts are far from me."*[91] It is these *charismatic* preachers persuade their flock, in a mastery of the language and flattering words that they have an exclusive channel to the rewards of heaven as those crying with their outstretched arms from the Rameumptum[92] of their *great and spacious buildings.*[93]

These words are very effective and attract the attention of many as the *philosophies of man mingled with scripture* litter the earth as stray ornaments of rubbish. There are some parts of the world where Christianity is not even recognized and in those places there are plenty of "distractions"[94] to go around, diverting all attention away from the one thing that will bring peace to the hearts of man.

For example, there are around 21 major world religions today[95]. Of the 33% of the world population which is Christian[96] there are 40,000 denominations within that one sect. There are plenty of things to believe (including nothing at all) to attract the interest of anyone and everyone.

Those who seek **truth** are met with an onslaught of information that would make the world's largest and most sophisticated super computer choke under the deluge of

---

[91] JSH 1:19
[92] Sherem, Jacob 7:4
[93] Alma 31:22
[94] See Chapter 29: Destractions…
[95] http://answers.yahoo.com/question/index?qid=1005120500015
[96] ditto

data. To seek an intellectual understanding of the matter would necessitate a lifetime of weighing the varying opinions to where none could sustain mortality for a fraction of time necessary to disseminate the varying points and counterpoints. Where would one go for answers?

This is the question that the enemy of God would like a seeker of truth to keep asking himself forever until it is too late for it to make any difference. As a result, the world is filled with philosophy and philosophers. Each of these come armed with worldly credentials certifying themselves as experts in the field who are willing and eager to persuade you that they are right in their infinite differences of understanding while standing on solid basis of fact and circumstance.

You will be reminded that you are lacking in the higher learning necessary to understand such difficult and intricate principles and that they will direct you in the way you should go. If you are spiritually minded, you may be directed toward a faith that meets your social needs mixed in with some philosophy, or maybe even some theology.

If the study of theology (theory) does not suit you, doctrine may be introduced and touted as fact. If you accept, you are welcomed into the group so long as you do not ask too many questions because answers are often presented as "mysteries" not revealed to men by a omnipotent God who created man so that they may serve to worship Him.

As the understanding of the creator is diluted into a swamp of confusion and contention it is nearly a guarantee that bewilderment will follow. Such was the case of a young pure hearted boy when he entered the woods one spring morning of 1820 to ask the source of all knowledge what he should do. The events that followed changed the history of a nation and the lives of millions of people who have embraced the work.

For his declaration of the facts, the boy was mocked, persecuted and eventually martyred for refusing to recant his proclamation to the world of the restoration of the fullness of the gospel at his hand as Prophet of God. It is interesting however that an affirmation of this fact comes to the heart of man, not through the intellect of enlightened minds of the trained intellect but through the whisper of a *still small voice*[97] in the heart with *pure intent*.[98]

In fact, the intellectual minds of the world have amassed a mountain of "facts" discrediting the individuals associated with the restoration and establishment of The Church of Jesus Christ of Latter Day Saints. Anyone with the power to *reason* would surely study the material which has been carefully prepared by the enemies of the church in certified, notarized and sworn triplicate to "prove" its validity…but nothing that can be written can suppress the power of the third member of the Godhead, The Holy Ghost.

He is present whenever truth is being taught[99] and will affirm truth to whomever seeks it. In the words of "the Grinch (who stole Christmas)[100] "That is something that

---

[97] D&C 85:6
[98] Moroni 10:8
[99] Ensign Mar 1997, Teaching and Learning by the Spirit
[100] Dr Suess

simply must not happen" so long as there are those who seek your support by priest craft.

By not embracing the self-declaring definition of Christianity, you become labeled as one "outside" the anointed faith and not admitted into the club of publicly recognized and acceptable religions. Such behavior is akin to a "club" refusing to elitist children taller, darker, wider or different than they. Would the loving God they profess to embrace or condone such behavior?

It appears to me that the Christian distinction is determined by none other than the Lord Himself. This determination is made by the condition of the heart and not on the narrow confines involved in the strict and generally accepted understanding of the Trinity.

Contention and division in and among the Christian faith would be a desirable condition for the adversary as confusion, distrust and disbelief follows. *"Behold my house is a house of order saith the Lord God and not a house of Confusion."[101]*

For there to be no confusion there can only be one voice, a voice of clarity, certainty and absolution. At no other time in the history of man did this condition exist than at the time the Savior Himself walked the streets of Jerusalem.

In the modern city of Bethlehem, there are no fewer than a dozen places that claim to be the birthplace of Jesus Christ. Certainly a modern day example where, *"There are*

---

[101] D&C 132:8

many that say lo here and others that say lo there."[102] The "conclusion is confusion."

The Bible does in fact have an answer for this dilemma: *"If any of you lack wisdom, let him ask of God."[103]* With this restoration came the fulfillment of Amos 3:7: *"Surely the Lord God will do nothing, but. He revealeth his secret unto his servants the prophets."* The purpose of the restoration of Prophets and apostles are to serve as special witness to the children of God and to clarify His work.

As you sit on the hillside in the Mount of Olives and look over the modern city of Jerusalem the confusion is blatantly obvious. The city is divided in four different sections: Arab, Christian, Jewish and Armenian. The Muslim call for prayer is broadcast from loudspeakers and heard for a mile away for all sections to hear regardless of their religious persuasion.

Can you imagine how the world could benefit from one single voice from God to mankind......The word of a prophet?

> *"O Jerusalem, Jerusalem, thou that killest*
> *the prophets and stonest them which are sent*
> *unto thee. How often would I have gathered*
> *thy children together even as a hen gathereth*
> *her chickens under her wings, and ye would not."[104]*

---

[102] JSH
[103] James 1:5
[104] Matt 23:37:

In the pure and simple truths left from the modern translation of the Bible[105] the world would be wiser to understand, "that it is through small and simple things that the Lord establishes his works."[106] It is not in the majesty of the pontiffs cloths, the ornamentation of the cathedrals or the mastery of architecture of Notre Dam that the glory of God is manifested, it is in the hearts and deeds of His servants as they listen to the promptings of the Holy Ghost and embrace the fullness of the Gospel in spite of those worldly men declaring foul.

Heavenly Father loves all of His children. He *"giveth to all men liberally and abradeth not."*[107] Inasmuch as the *"spirit giveth light to every man"*[108] the Holy Ghost is present whenever the true doctrine of Jesus Christ is being taught. The spirit is manifesting the truth of Christ's mission on earth to all of Gods children wherever they may be in the world. Those who receive His message and act apply it to their lives will be greatly blessed.

The power of God is within each of us along with the power to find Him. It is only a prayer away.[109] If you are not interested in the power of prayer and the personal revelation it can bring, remember there will always be someone willing to preach to you!

---

[105] Gen Conf 1984, The Simplicity of Gospel Truths
[106] Alma 37:6
[107] James 1:5
[108] D&C 84:46
[109] Moroni 10:4

Truth, Acquired#: 31
Given the chance, the Lord will make us better people.

SOMETHING OLD, SOMETHINGNEW

Ten years seems like a long time. This is the tenure I anticipated serving when I was called into the Stake presidency. We were a brand new Stake formed from two adjoining ones with regions expanding into the northern end of the state. It was hard to provide the services needed for an area that included rural and metro suburban areas.

I was excited to be in the service of my God and pleased to devote my life to building up the kingdom. At times, I felt that it would never end. However, as the Presidency began to build the outline of the Stake's position and personality, we went to work. The months drifted into years and we soon found ourselves facing the reality that our time was becoming short.

I was informed of the receipt of the release letter one month prior to its effective date. The idea of leaving the position was unattractive to say the least. Though the time required was demanding and the efforts were challenging at times, I knew I would miss my association with the youth of the Stake and the souls we were called to serve. I had become involved in their lives and grew to love them. I accepted my release with dread. However, the Lord dealt with me kindly in a very simple way.

I was sitting in my usual place on the stand during Stake Conference when the names of our replacements were called for a sustaining vote. It was at that moment that I heard their names for the first time. As I saw them approach the stand to take their newly appropriate space, I received the spirit of confirmation knowing that the Lords will had taken place. The Stake was in good hands. The Lord knew its needs and sat worthy men in place to meet the challenges that would follow.

It was interesting that during the weeks and months that followed, my heart was calm with the confirming spirit of acceptance for our work. The Lord had accepted it and blessed us with the opportunity to sit again with our wives and families.

The concepts of "old" versus "new" are mentioned many times in the scriptures. *"Old things are done away and all things have become new."*[110] Yes, I had become an "old" one and it was necessary to introduce the "new." This concept was reinforced by my state of mind and communication from the joints of my body that it was time to step aside and let a new pair of limbs fill the chair.

---

[110] 3 Nephi 12:47

The doctrine of old vs new is used several more times in the Bible and Book of Mormon.

- Old wine is not put into new bottles. Mark 2:22, Matthew 9:17, Luke 5: 37
- A new garment is not placed "upon an old." Luke 5:6
- No man having drunk old wine desireth new. Luke 5:39

These along with many others, outline the complete understanding the Lord has of human nature and what is needed to further His work. There comes a time to move on, to experience new things and give others the opportunity to learn as we have. Maybe this is why we are rarely held in the same position in the church for very long. Maybe this is why we are called to the position we feel least qualified to serve, so we can become qualified by performing the task.

The ordinance of Baptism also symbolizes this change from old to new. As the person is submerged into the water and raised, it symbolizes the death and the resurrection, the *old* you and the *new* you and your acceptance of Christ's atonement delivering you from the earth to the Heavenly realm. Our birth delivers us from the old existence to the new. We learn and grow as we progress from one person to another.

As we grow, learn and progress, we advance beyond the state we were before and become new, improved and better thereby providing the need for the "old things" to "be done away."[111] It is for this reason that we should never be reluctant to look within ourselves for ways to improve from our *old ways* that may be hindering our growth.

Some of us may feel familiarity with the geological definition of "old" as being "reduced through erosion and weathering." This certainly applies to me. The sharp edges of my youth filled with ambition, drive and the will to advance have been reduced the smooth edges of a stone taken from a fast moving river after relentless, endless and ruthless opposition. Like the rock, I felt lucky to hold my spot on the bottom, much less advance against the current. Of course, this analogy is not intended to deny the ability to overcome any and all opposition only to illustrate what many of us feel.

In many ways, old is descriptive of very good things that should be embraced. If *old* refers to individual or family values entrenched in Gospel principles, they should never be abandoned. If *old* refers to a legacy of generational faith in the restored Gospel, it should be cherished. It is important that we take this concept in the proper context as the Lord has taught the principle.

- In speaking of the Law of Moses, the old was put away and the new law implemented. [112]
- In connection with purpose of the earth, it will eventually pass away and become new. [113]

---

[111] 3 Nephi 12:47
[112] 3 Nephi 15:2
[113] D&C 29:24

- The *old* mortal body will die and become new[114]
- Jerusalem, "had been in a time of old, but it shall be built up again."[115]
- The covenant of marriage was becoming the "new and everlasting" covenant.[116]

While considering all of these attributes it is easy to surmise that the purpose of the earth is to change us from old to new physically and spiritually. With this *new* condition we can stand beside our Lord and King in eternal exaltation where nothing exists but eternal principles that have created all we know to exist. Eternal principles do not change with politics or the whims of a human society. They are what they are. Their existence is eternal and that makes them old. They may become new only as we discover them for the first time. Though they have always been there they are not new, they never will be because they always *were.*

It is human arrogance to believe that we have the ability to control the environment that surrounds us. Though we may be able to vote on civil rights and privileges, we cannot vote on the law of physics which holds the universe together.

All of us have experiences where we see the changes the Gospel makes in the lives of people. During my calling as a Ward Mission leader, we were privileged to have an investigator who was found while tracting in the

---

[114] D&C 29: 25
[115] Ether 13:5
[116] D&C 22:1

public housing area of our ward. He was a tall skinny black man who first attended church in ragged jeans and a partially dismantled "t" shirt. He was a good soul who had little opportunity in life to advance beyond his original social status. He was extremely shy and quiet.

As he continued to embrace the message of Jesus Christ, a noticeable change took place. It was obvious in every way. His rags changed to business attire and eventually a suit, complete with a white shirt and tie. He would comb his hair and polish his shoes. His personality changed and he became more sociable and comfortable in his surroundings. The restored Gospel of Jesus Christ had changed this good man from the *old* that he was to the *new,* a disciple, and a follower of the Savior. This is a mighty change that happens upon a soul for body and spirit that can only take place by the Master's hand. This man is surely the living example of the scripture, "And thus they become new creatures..."[117]

This *new creature* is literally snatched from the jaws of poverty, inherited by the world of circumstances where there is no easy exit, to a greater understanding of personal worth and purpose. To be a son or daughter of God is a realization of personal worth that transcends the sinful ambitions and messages of the world that teach that happiness is obtained by fame and wealth.

In high school, I was on the committee to plan our graduation. In the closing prayer, that I was privileged to have written, I included the famous words of prayer, "God,

---

[117] Mosiah 27:28

grant me the serenity to accept the things I cannot change, the courage to change the things I can and the wisdom to know the difference."[118] We may not be able to change anyone else, but we can certainly change ourselves.

There are good and bad things associated with both words, old and new. The Lord has given us both and a mind to work through the challenges of life. Our outlook and prospects for the future should always be fresh, *new* and exciting to us. While it may be the *old* ways that bring us happiness and joy, our renewed endurance against the temptations of the world will forever be our companion as we stand before the judgment bar of God.

As members of the Church of Jesus Christ of Latter-Day Saints, we rejoice in the message that God lives and stands at the head of our church. We invite all souls to enter the kingdom and witness the mighty change that can take place transfiguring our old selves to the new. The new one will celebrate who we are and what we can become. We delight in doing good and enjoy being an instrument in the hands of the Lord. The transition of mankind from the blood and sins of the world to the eternal happiness associated with exaltation associated with eternal families and eternal progression is the goal.

With the knowledge this eternal message brings, who among us would not shout with joy as did Ammon saying, *"I do not boast in my own strength, nor in my own wisdom: but behold, my joy is full, yea, my heart is brim*

---

[118] American Theologian: Reinhold Niebuhr (1892-1971)

with joy and I will rejoice in my God. "[119] Wasn't this the
same Ammon that was fighting the church with Alma, the
son of Mosiah?

> *"Now the sons of Mosiah were numbered*
> *among the unbelievers, and all one of the sons*
> *of Alma was numbered among them, he being*
> *called Alma after his father; nevertheless he*
> *became a very wicked and an idolatrous man.*
> *And he was a man of many words and he did*
> *speak much flattery to the people; therefore he*
> *led many of the people to do after the manner*
> *of his iniquities.* "[120]

There is no greater example of the change that can
take place under the Lord's direction as took place with all
that were in Alma's company that fateful day when He
intervened to change their path. The *old* were wicked; the
new became instruments of God to change the course of the
history and provide one of the most colorful transition
stories in all of the writings of the prophets; *"but with God
all things are possible."* [121]

This is a message we should take to heart when we
consider giving up or entertain the notion that we have
come too far or are too far gone to change. These words are
those used by Satan to discourage us from beginning the

---

[119] Alma 26:11
[120] Mosiah 27"8
[121] Matt 19:26

change from old to new. The *New* embraces light, joy and happiness and the company of God. With this understanding it should be easier to perform the "spring cleaning" of our souls and,

> *"Put on the new man which is renewed in knowledge after the image of him that created him: Where there is neither Greek nor Jew, circumcision nor uncircumcision, Barbarian, Scyhthian, bond nor free: but Christ is all, an in all."[122]*

Wow, that's a change.

---

[122] Colossians 3: 10-11

SECTION 5

As Understanding Becomes Certain

"Dealing with the more complex issues"

As we accumulate life experiences, our level of understanding grows to a level of knowledge which becomes "certainty." We have matured but still in need of further enlightenment. We submit ourselves to the will of the Lord and are anxious to serve him in every way. In this condition we can serve as only a seasoned servant can.

Truth, Certain #: 32
God's knowledge and understanding
is complete and perfect.

THE LORD KNOWS

(Predestination or perfect understanding?)

The discussion of predestination often comes up in Gospel discussion. Jeremiah was told that the Lord knew him before he was.[123] The debate usually centers on the concept of *agency*, if we were predestined to do a certain thing or fulfill a certain calling, how are we then able to exercise choice when we are "destined" to it? It seems to conflict with the plan of salvation. The Lord gives us direction and instruction but we are free to choose for ourselves. *"And we will prove them herewith to see if they*

---

[123] Jer 1:5

will do all things whatsoever the Lord their God shall command them. "[124]

Likewise, foreordination has similar connotation; how can we be ordained for something that is contingent on our worthiness if we have yet to prove our worthiness? When considering the conundrum, most turn away and write it off as "one of those things" that we will understand *later*. As do many of us, we filter the questions of life through the things we can understand and come in contact with regularly.

Since I was a boy, and had the strength to pick up a stick, I wanted a gun. The first ones were usually sticks with a "cool" handle or a long piece of slender wood. Being raised on a farm, there was always a need to have a firearm handy. My dad would quickly reach for the rifle over the mantle to protect the cattle from the feral dogs or coyotes. There was always the need to supplement our family meal with game naturally provided by the land.

I loved to go hunting with my dad in the forest behind our house to look for small game that we could bring home for the evening meal. When I was old enough to gain the trust of my dad, I was given my first rifle, a 22 caliber long rifle. Countless rounds were sent hurtling down its rifled barrel toward various inert targets of opportunity. There was no off color leaf, or unusual protrusion from a tree that was safe from my attentive gaze.

Often, I would send a round glancing off the surface of the family pond that would redirect its path with a

---

[124] Abr 3:25

whistle and a most satisfying sound. Where did it go, I would ask? With the closest neighbor out of range, it was luckily not a problem. Still, I thought, it would be awesome, if I could find the misshaped bullet lodged in the side of a tree or on the ground at the end of its multidirectional trajectory, it would have a tale to tell; it would be a great souvenir.

The love of firearms has never left me. I have collected many and am now in possession of the precious Browning 12 gauge shotgun my dad had when I was a child. Since then, with my time in the military and with my own farm, I have honed my skills in the art.

Usually, an individual that does a lot of shooting will invest in the equipment to reload his own ammunition. It greatly reduces the cost and allows the shooter to customize the rounds to meet his specific needs. With the study of this exercise comes the understanding of ballistics. Each caliber has many different recipes. With the combination of brass (casings), projectiles (bullets), powder (propellant) and primers (igniter), you can create a round that will perform as you wish.

As you can imagine, there are many combinations of these ingredients that will each make a difference in the performance of the round. Each bullet has a shape and weight that will perform differently. The burn rate of the powder is different. The characteristics of the primer are all combined to match the characteristics of each to create the flight path of the projectile that will most accurately hit the designated target.

To make it even more interesting, it seems that each rifle has its own personality, its own fingerprint or personality. Rounds that perform in one rifle may behave quite differently in another of the same caliber. It is just "one of those things" that makes the sport fun and challenging.

To achieve the desired effect, we have to plan and experiment with each of these combinations. We have to send the fired projectile through a chronograph to measure its speed. Once we know the speed and its weight, we can determine the ballistic coefficient. With the coefficient in hand, we can determine the "foot pound of energy" and the trajectory (the flight path). We can determine its path in inches; where it will be in relation to the barrel at any point within its path to where and when it falls to the earth.

These ballistic tables have been developed over a long period of time taking countless samples from countless rounds to create an understanding of how these individual components relate to each other. Because the bullets are shaped differently, have different propellants, are sent down range with different speeds and angle to the earth's gravitational field, there are truly infinite resulting possibilities. To be able to calculate exactly where and when each of these rounds can be found on the ground after their high speed ride is unimaginable. However, is it impossible to God?

In several scriptures we hear the phrase *sands of the sea.* The implication is that they are each numbered and known unto God. *"Are not two sparrows sold for a farthing? and one of them shall not fall on the ground without your Father."*[125] This familiar scripture seems to be understandable to us until we consider how many sparrows there are, ever have been or ever will be on the earth. So how much greater attention does He place on His sons and daughters? *"For behold, this is my work and my glory to bring to pass the immortality and eternal life of man."*[126] With this doctrine, we know that His children are his first and only priority, so how much more important are they than a sparrow?

How difficult is it to imagine then that He knows each of us by name considering how many of us there are? *"If I should count them, they are more in number than the sand: when I awake, I am still with thee."*[127] With the same reasoning as mentioned before, is not this level of understanding and mental capability impossible? The calculation seems to be beyond the capability of the earth's most sophisticated super computer, but it is true.

Our Heavenly Father is capable of unimaginable thought. He understands every aspect of the universe and each of its individual ingredients, how they behave separately and collectively. His understanding of EVERY discipline of academia is perfect. *"Dost thou know that balancing of the clouds, the wondrous works of him which is perfect in knowledge?"*[128] With this knowledge and *honor* with the elements of the cosmos, He created man, the earth and the universe of which we marvel.

---

[125] Matt 10: 29
[126] Moses 1:39
[127] PS139:18
[128] Job 37:16

As we were sent to this earth from His presence, He knew our *weight*, our *caliber*, our *propellant* and how we would be sent downrange into the fabric of life. With each challenge we would have a trajectory that may alter our flight path depending on *what we were made of*. With known ingredients, speed and flight path, our relative destiny and proximity for landing could be understood and isolated. But with God, it would be perfect... a perfect understanding.

Imagine in following graphic, the bullet which represents us (our character) being fired into a forest of iron trees which represents challenges, trials and choices. Each tree could be shaped differently and have different reflective tendencies. They could be placed in different proximities to each other with infinite possibilities. As the bullet entered, its properties (motivation) are known. Its flight time is predetermined (life span) by God; its exact direction into the forest (place/family/location) is known by God by identifying the *ballistic coefficient*.

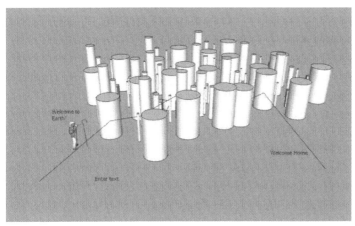

With a perfect understanding of a God relating to every law of physics and related disciplines, He would know exactly how each tree (trial) would deflect the path and how it would react because of its unique inherent properties. Once the flight path had exhausted the predetermined life span, God in His infinite wisdom, would be able to walk on the seashore of life and pick up the individual projectile from all others, hold it in His hand, call you by name and say "Welcome Home."

Heavenly Father knew us before we were sent, *"Before I formed thee in the belly I knew thee; and before thou camest forth out of the womb I sanctified thee, and I ordained thee a prophet unto the nations."*[129] Also, it would appear there were some of those spirits that were different than the rest, perhaps a "larger caliber" than the rest of us. There were those among us who were great.

---

[129] Jer 1:5

"I observed that they were also among the noble and great ones who were chosen in the beginning to be rulers in the church of God."[130]

With this infinite knowledge, our Heavenly Father knew where we would be and when. He knew our personality, our family situation and how each person would relate to each other because He understood all principles associated with each infinite interchange, a perfect understanding. With this knowledge He would be able to ordain those who would be called on earth to be our leaders.

Most of us can rehearse a story in our lives where we were at a particular place and at a particular time that seemed to be an incredible coincidence. The situation presented itself only after a series of unlikely events occurred to generate the result. The effect of this result presented opportunities for jobs, relationships or teaching moments that were of great benefit to us. Is it beyond comprehension to believe that the Lord orchestrated the events for His divine purposes?

Being raised in Georgia, I became a southern son in my very identity. Through a series of seemingly random and often apparent unfortunate events, I moved to the panhandle of Florida. At the time, it felt to be the right thing to do but its purpose was illusive.

Looking back now, I can see how the Lord was instrumental in orchestrating this event. My experience there positively affected my spiritual growth that could

---

[130] D&C 138:55

have never occurred in any other way. The Lord knew this. He knew the circumstances I was facing and all of the factors, people and conditions that would have interaction. He added direction to my life that helped me become a better servant, father and husband. Although the things leading up to the experience were painful, it was necessary for the event to take place and beneficial for me and my family overall.

Similar stories fill the history books of early church development regarding Joseph's move to Palmyra following an unfortunate financial reversal for the family. Joseph was moved within walking distance of the buried golden plates as the Lord had a perfect understanding of the circumstances that would take place. Though the capability is beyond our imagination, it is possible, *"with God all things are possible."[131]* It is not predestination; it is the perfect understanding of the Lord!

---

[131] Matt 19:26

Truth, Certain #: 33
  The intellect of *reason* can be twisted
  to harm the nature of faith.

REASON VS FAITH

Being raised in the South, I have been confronted by friends from other faiths asking about the crazy things they have heard about the *Mormons.* You know the drill, "How many wives do you have? Do you have your own *Bible*," And let's not forget the age old challenge to our membership in the family of Christianity. The delusion, illusion and confusion of information, or misinformation continue to flow from the father of all lies in incessant streams of bewilderment. After all, isn't this his goal?

  In direct contrast to the Lord's house of order, [132] Satan's plan is to have disorder in our house, and he is extremely organized in the process. It is a paradox in

---

[132] D&C 88:119

design but skillfully structured. Our enemy would give us no option but to follow him as he removed the *honor* from God Himself. To understand this concept is to have a better understanding of ourselves, our surroundings and the historical events of our past.

It has long been the strategy of those designers combating the growth of the restored gospel, to illustrate in great detail the early struggles of the church as the members dealt with the unthinkable injustice they were required to bare. They were persecuted, driven and even slain by instruments of hate, prejudice and jealously. However, as in all conflicts, "to the *victors* go the spoil."

As the saints flew from their persecutors, those left with the pen and script created the reality according to their best interest. From a historical point of view, these observations are usually not exactly representative of reality. These same historical accounts are today being propagated by the naysayers to discredit the intentions of the divine purpose of the Kingdom of God. This knowledge is in itself a witness of the reality of the evil origins of the disinformation as it is hurled toward every inquiring investigator like a javelin in the heart of conversion.

It is therefore appropriate to ask the question, "Why, why does the Lord allow this process to continue?" Those who have fully accepted the Gospel in their lives and have received a spiritual manifestation to its truthfulness, know beyond a shadow of a doubt that it is true; all of it! After receiving this witness through the power of the Holy Ghost, they want to share the "good news" with all that they love and care about. It always seems to be the case however, when that newly taught soul seeks for answers they will find many who are willing to teach them; *teach them about the Mormons.*

It is almost always dipped in the flavor of contention leaving a taste of confusion and despair. Let us make no mistake that this message is also accompanied by a spirit, a different spirit however. It is the spirit contrary to that of the Holy one but that one who would destroy you and your desire to find the truth.

It is easy in every circumstance in life to find countless opinions on every subject under the sun. Experts will take the witness stand, sworn under oath, and take completely opposing views on a particular subject, each claiming superior credentials to the other.

The Prophet Joseph experienced this phenomenon in his early quest for the truth,

> *"Good feelings of both the priests and the converts were more pretended than real for a scene of great confusion and bad feeling ensued- priest contending against priest, and convert against convert; so that all their good feelings one for another, if they ever had any, were entirely lost in a strife of works and a contest about opinions."[133]*

It was confusion and contention that fed the engine of deception. This is the exact same tactic used by the evil

---

[133] JSH 1:6

one, the father of lies. The problem persists today as he leads many precious souls away from the choicest blessings on earth. More often than not, the early events of the history of the church are used to discredit its truth as it has been propagated though the enemies of the church since that very day.

In the south, we call it "anti"; that material especially designed to confuse and contend. It is deliberately used to prevent further investigation though the use of false and twisted information. Yet it continues.

During my lifetime of experiencing these phenomena, I have come to understand the difference between Faith and Reason. With all of the *anti,* material available to anyone who has the desire, why would anyone join such a group? It describes a pretty despicable lot of misguided people who will not take the time to think for themselves!

But alas, opposition is necessary in all things. Without opposition there would be no faithfulness.[134] Faith gives us a basis to make a decision in spite of the *reasons* portrayed in this misinformation while those who demand that spirituality must fit in the realm of reason weigh all view points and proceeds rationally. These are those who fall into the intellectual trap of the *enlightened* who seek *truth* without regard for right and wrong.

Reason, gives everyone plausible rationality to deny the truth and harden their hearts against spiritual promptings. To me, this sounds like a perfect scenario for

[134] 2 Nephi 2:11

the earthly test we are facing at this moment, to sift out the wheat from the tares.

With this being understood, is it also likely that Heavenly Father allowed some of these most controversial characters and circumstances of the history of the church to fulfill this very purpose? If that were the case, one with *reason* in their motive for conversion would have to join in the eternal family of God on earth in spite of their intellectual motive to the contrary.

True conversion originates from the heart not the head. An *intellectual* conversion will never stand against the scrutiny of a manipulative world. *"And after they had tasted of the fruit they were ashamed, because of those that were scoffing at them and they fell away into forbidden paths and were lost."[135]*

The person that gives his heart to the Lord would be a soul of great worth, placing the spiritual above the physical! These would be the type of individuals the Lord would have in His church leading, guiding and directing His saints, teaching His children and motivating His youth to do the right thing in spite of what their friends or the world may say. They would be the ones to stand for what they know is right, no matter what.

The process of true conversion is in fact a process of faith over reason. We have not seen God. We have not seen Christ or even the Holy Ghost but we know they exist by faith and the miracle that follows conversion.

---

[135] 1 Nephi 8:28

We live in a physical world where nothing can truly exist unless we can see it under a microscope or measure its effects by a windmill or paddlewheel. We are trained to be reasonable, rational and educated as we make decision, but the Lord says, "Listen to your heart." It is in your heart that you will find joy and joy is the eternal union of body and spirit.

Of course, in the realm of perfect knowledge, reason would take center stage in the basis for conversion, but where would be the test? *"For if you know a thing, why then"...*[136] And in most cases, the miracle of the mysteries of the gospel is only shared by the spirit after the manifestation of faith so until then, faith has precedence over reason in the conversion process of the mortal man. Faith precedes the miracle.[137] Sooooo....bring it on, our faith is sufficient! There is a *reason* for our *faith.*

---

[136] Alma 32:35
[137] Adney Y. Komatsu, Gen Conf 10-1979

Truth, Certain#: 34

**Betrayal can be the most
painful emotional experience in life.**

ANATOMY OF BETRAYAL

No emotion can elicit more impact on the psyche of a person than that of betrayal. Having once loved and trusted someone and to have them transform from an ally to advisory is to cut through the "center" of our soul. The examples contained in the history of human experience are truly endless. In most cases, there are examples in our own lives that are much too unpleasant to discuss. The prevailing question from the offended seems to be "why?" In most cases it can be explained simply as selfishness, greed or pride.

Each has a basis of understanding all to its own, most of which highlights the more pleasant tendencies of human nature. As the betrayer flees with the perceived victory, the victims are left in the shattered remains and the luminescent dust cloud of the destructive event.

In most cases, we are caught unawares of the plot and left with our inability to make sense of it all. The fact is that in most cases, it does not make any sense. We only know that we were betrayed which limits our ability to ever release our tender and vulnerable feelings of trust again.

The betrayer has moved on without us, often using us as a springboard to advance their life's agenda. The biggest mistake we make in these circumstances is to "try to understand." The process is usually torturous and unproductive. We simply need to recognize the fact that we were bitten by a predator and must quietly remove the venom from our blood stream and move on with our lives. They are no longer worthy of our trust; they have changed. We can take comfort in the fact that there are things in life that are stable and permanent; the behavior of mankind is not one of them.

The possibility that those we once loved and trusted "have changed" is one option to consider, possibly the one that gives us the most comfort. Otherwise, we would have to admit that we misjudged them; our discernment process was faulty or maybe we never knew them at all. This personal admission is often unacceptable as it highlights a flaw in us. We are the victim, we did nothing wrong...right?

I am familiar with a situation where two couples were best friends and regularly socialized together. During the years of friendship, they would enter each other's home with any casualness offered any family member. The adult male of the family friend *crossed the line* with his best friend's daughter. Of course, what followed was heartache, anger and a desire for vengeance. I was close to both of the families and respected and love each of them. It was a very painful process to work through and continued for a long time.

We helped him struggle through the repentance process. He faced the full disciplinary process of the church and began an immediate "come back" to full fellowship. He was loved by the members who went out of their way to show him support and fellowship. He was embraced in tears by those who offered him love and counsel. This display was in the spirit of forgiving and love as taught by the Savior. However, there was an unintended consequence that few recognized.

Among all of this flow of kindness shown toward the perpetrator, the victim was overlooked. She felt that she was being ignored. The victim's father was inconsolable. He left his wife, his family and his home. The victim's mother was devastated and heartbroken. Not only was she betrayed by the friend that she opened her heart and home to, she felt their family was victimized again. Where was the stream of love and support she had witnessed for the offender that destroyed her life?

The details of the disciplinary council are always confidential. No one outside the room where it is administered can witness the tears of pain and the agony associated being formally separated with God. It is natural to want to do everything possible to bring them back. In contrast, the victims have done nothing wrong. Their blessings are completely intact. There is nothing to discuss except what is going to happen to the offender, which cannot be talked about; it is confidential; herein lyes the leader's dilemma.

What can you say to a young lady who has been forced to deal with such a horrible thing? How can you explain the egress behavior of the wrongdoer? Bishops have little training on counseling, especially for this. As a result, they go about the mechanics of doing what they do know. They work through the disciplinary process as outlined in the Handbook of Instructions.

The situation is commensurate with the story of the Prodigal Son. In the end, the message is clear, *"Son, Thou are ever with me and all that I have is thine. It was meet that we should make merry and be glad for this thy brother was dead and is alive again and was lost and is found."*[138]

It is essential that the victims remember this counsel. They have lost nothing while the offender has lost everything. It may not feel that way, but it is the truth. The message of the story is the need for the leaders to show enormous support to the victim's family. They should meet with them very regularly to give love, support and counsel, even if they say that they do not need it.

It will be a struggle for the victim to fight off the temptation to seek reprisal. The Lord has a system to deal with these matters and it should be allowed to take its course. The Lord has appointed Judges of Israel. This is the Bishops calling. Our calling as members is to seek the love

---

[138] Luke 15:31,32

and light of God and draw strength from Him. Though this is easier said than done, with faith and prayer all hearts can be healed.

I once had a friend that I considered a true brother. We became very close through the years as we shared our experiences in dealing with the challenges of life, family and career. We would give counsel to each other as we faced these challenges and felt the spirit of the Holy Ghost in our discussions of the Gospel and the fulfillment of our separate callings. I felt that we understood each other in a way that only a brother could.

Then one day, something happened; he changed. My friend took a job out of town and over the course of months; he abandoned his wife, children, family and faith. I sat in his living room with him and his wife as she pled with him to *come home* to all that he knew to be true. I could feel the cold in his countenance as he spiritually, emotionally and then physically turned away. His sweet wife wept as I watched him enter their family sedan and drive toward his new life and another woman. The man I once knew was gone and I would not see him again.

After many years, the betrayed companion never came to grips with what happened. Bitterness became the companion that filled in the void of her life. She did not deserve the hand she had been dealt. She did no wrong but found herself among those who struggle with the circumstances of life resulting from misdirected choices or just bad luck. It simply was not fair.

As I have struggled with the emotional loss of my friend, I wonder: Is it possible that I never really knew him at all? The man I knew would never have been capable of doing what he did. To have "changed" so drastically is not in the nature of the devoted priesthood holder I knew.

To have changed or revealing the true nature of oneself are both real possibilities. In the end, it really does not matter. The Lord has created this earth for this divine purpose; to determine who we are and what we are capable of becoming. It is a test to see what we are made of, how we will react and what choices we will make.

At one point in our lives, all of us face this eventuality. We open our hearts to those we love. Our innermost feelings are shared exposing our souls and the tender core of our identity. All of the defensive walls of emotion have been willfully lowered to those we trust. Betrayal is the process of deliberately leveraging this trust to do us harm. It is treachery, infidelity, disloyalty and the contrary to the promises made to God and to each other.

Often the self-evaluation process following the event is self-critical and destructive. We expect to have been blessed with clairvoyance to detect the defective character flaw before it is manifested. The personal expectation of our deductive reasoning is unrealistic and beyond our capability but Satan stirs up the guilt in us, lying that it was done because "we deserve it" or "we had it coming." It is also a circumstance that would draw upon the darker potential of our character to "get even," to retaliate which festers into a destructive frenzy of self-annihilation where nothing is gained.

Betrayal is an effective tool of the advisory to break down individuals, families and communities. It was the tool used to deliver the God of this world to the most painful mortal death designed by humanity.

It happens because we have the freedom to choose; it is God's gift to us. We cannot alter the decision process of others beyond their will. It is a fact of life and one that we need to understand as a child of God.

Our comfort and solace is received by understanding that our Heavenly Father is conscious of all. He has a perfect understanding of our thoughts, feelings, ambitions and intentions. He knows our hearts and those around us. He has placed all of us here to prove ourselves and to determine if we are worthy of His presence after these earthly decisions are made.

Betrayal of the righteous will certainly bring condemnation. There will be no act of evil that will not be dealt with by our Father who created us. In the end the only concern of ours should be our relationship with our Heavenly Father; how did we conduct ourselves during this personal trial? Did we remain faithful in our thoughts and deeds? Did we turn the other cheek[139] and proceed with doing righteousness continually?

There are those among us who are better at this than most. Simply put, we need to "let go." What has happened has happened. If we are the victim, we are innocent; let's keep it that way. We need to learn from it (to whatever futile endeavor it may be) and move forward and remove the venom of the predator from our blood stream.

---

[139] Matt 5:39

Again, the doctrine is the source of comfort and solace. We should submerse ourselves in the doctrine of Jesus Christ and surround ourselves in good people that we love and trust.

As we look into the eyes of the innocent children, we see God and His love for us and His desire that we all return to Him as an eternal family for the eternities. No amount of deception, deceit, lies or betrayal should keep us from this eternal goal. All of these tools of Satan should be recognized for what they are and avoided as a plaque of humanity. Our Eternal Father loves us and wants us to come home in righteousness. Let's make that happen.

No one who has ever lived has been betrayed with greater notoriety than our Savior Jesus Christ. If there is an example to follow on the matter it is Him. At the height of His suffering and the culmination of his pain and humiliation he said, *"Forgive them father for they know not what they do."*[140] Is it a ridiculous notion to expect one of us to have similar sentiments? Maybe, but it should be our goal. It is hard for me to believe that anyone would choose to face the consequences of offence toward men or God. They are eternal.

---

[140] Luke 23:34

HOW DO I FORGIVE?

(Sometimes it's not so easy)

It was a Sunday just like any other. A new family was scheduled to speak for the first time and introduce themselves to the ward family. I was visiting my home ward as a high councilman and was happy to be in attendance with family for a change. The new sister was an attractive young wife and mother and sat on the stand with reverence and dignity awaiting her turn to address the congregation.

Her message was simple, direct and very eloquently delivered. Following her spiritual message, she began to give some history on herself and family. In a very *matter of fact* tone, she announced that she was a victim of incest at the hands of her father as a youth and was suffering from the mental challenges associated with that abuse.

I was amazed at her candor and honesty. It was not said in a way to solicit sympathy or pity. She did not condemn anyone in her words. It was as if she simply desired to make her situation public as if she was confiding with members of her family. She recognized that the experience made her different. She said that she would seem aloof and distracted at times but wanted everyone to know that they should not take any of these things personally. It was simply something she was working through and wanted us to know that she wanted to be a part of the Ward.

Following the Sacrament Meeting, there was a brief outpouring of love and concern by a few in attendance. However, from that time forward, this good sister, and her family, was avoided and shunned. Their presence was not long in the area as they moved away within a short period of time.

Being out of the Ward on assignment a lot, I was not directly involved on the degrading condition of their fellowship by my brothers and sisters but was in fear of it following that day. It is just one of those subjects that you don't know what to say or how to handle.

What on earth do you say to a person like that, "I know how you feel? I'm so sorry? Or maybe, what actually happened?" These along with all other possible casual comments seem like petty platitudes paling in significance to the reality of the horror this sweet sister had experienced.

It's like being an unwilling witness to a brutal murder. You wish you had never seen it and want no part of it. Why would you disrupt your peaceful suburban lifestyle to the hurricane of evil, emotion and betrayal that this event and this sister represented? Unable to answer these questions, the logical solution is to "steer clear" of the situation all together. In this case, the innocent victim is "let out with the bath water."

Regretfully, another situation occurred in the Stake with an active family involving two daughters and an attending priesthood holder father. The circumstances were horrific and the shock wave launched in the community and local media ignited a fire storm of poisonous publicity. The resulting state of affairs is reminiscent of the tragic plane crashes that occur on occasion. It is the worst case scenario; no one survives.

It represents a total and complete failure on all accounts. It is the battle where every single soldier was killed in action. It is the submarine that implodes under the intense pressure of the ocean abyss with no time to signal distress. It is the rogue wave that capsizes the ship with no warning sending it to the depths of the sea.

The record books are filled with accounts of horrifying defeats at the hands of the NVA in Viet Nam, the Germans in WWII and the Japanese in the Pacific. In many cases, the rescuers came after the carnage was complete only to identify the bodies and notify the next of kin. Sometimes, things just go terribly wrong! That is what this situation reminds me of. All that is left is carnage and its affiliated documentation.

The average person does not know what to do, what to say or how to react in these situations. It is not they are prejudice, judgmental or rude; it is just a threat to their peaceful life which has enough stress on its own. This is a *load* that the average person is just not equipped to bear. They know that they could offer no helpful advice and certainly feel unqualified to offer any counsel. In most cases, this applies to the leaders as well.

Bishops, Branch Presidents and Stake Presidents are good honorable men with rare exception. They are not however, formally trained to deal with such severe emotional issues from the victim's point of view. As a result, the needed counsel is often overlooked hoping that the "Lord will provide."

It is these unthinkable situations that need to be addressed for the sake of the souls that are called upon to experience them. As leaders, we should never be afraid to walk with our brothers and sisters on any road they are called upon to walk no matter how uncomfortable it is; this is our job, our calling.

It is however in these most atrocious cases where the question of *how* to forgive is presented. We know that we are commanded to forgive, "vengeance is mine."[141] We are taught to forgive all man, "I the Lord will forgive whom I will forgive, but for you it is required to forgive all men."[142] We read these scriptures and hear the words from beloved leaders but the wrench in our gut remains to tear at our inner peace.

In many cases, the offender appears to be free from recourse or blame. He or she is skilled in the art of

---

[141] Romans 12:19
[142] D&C 64:10

deception and persuasion where you, the victim, are portrayed as an antagonizer or even a willing accomplice in the offense. This only furthers the insult and adds to the injury. It seems that everyone may be fooled but you.

In your effort to make the facts come to light, lines are crossed and conduct is compromised for the sake of the "ends justifying the means." Here in lies the problem; as we chase that venomous snake that just bit us into the brambles, its poison hastily enters our hearts with its heightened beat which hastens our own demise. There simply is no winner in this fight. The pursuit of the answer to the question of "how" remains elusive.

Like most everyone else, I have had the occasion to be betrayed and offended more times than I have seen the sun rise. After the cumulative weight of the hurt and pain becomes more that I could bare, a decision had to be made. Do I carry all of this to the point is breaks my back or dump it off in the ditch where it belongs? It is philosophical really!

I remember a Hollywood production many years ago that depicts a soldier betrayed by his country. His reprisal was to launch a series of nuclear bombs on populated cities if the truth surrounding the betrayal was not made known to the world. In the end, one betrayal was followed by another to where the soldiers had determined to execute the plan. The lead soldier turned to his accomplice that was now getting cold feet and reluctant to assist in the simultaneous "turning of the keys" to activate the launch. When challenged by the soldier to follow through on the plan, the now belligerent collaborator made

270

a poetic observation, to paraphrase, "The whole world may be filled with thieves and jerks but that is no reason to blow it all up."[143]

In an odd way, this statement has been a lot of comfort to me because I know this is true. The world is filled with a lot of sick people. I know many who would put me in those ranks as well. The bottom line is that we are just in no position to judge or accuse anyone of anything. We need to just take care of ourselves. If we fail to do this, we can become offenders and betrayers ourselves; this of course, is what Satan wants. He never wants us to let go or forgive. Revenge breeds contention and hate. This is the path that leads to pain and misery which are constant companions of he who persuades us not to forgive. It is however very prudent to identify where these predators, offenders (snakes) dwell so as to avoid them.

Forgiving them does not mean that we must submit ourselves to their further abuse. We must recognize them for what they are and let the Lord do the rest. If we know there are snakes in the garden, we do not walk in the tall grass barefooted. The answer to the question of "how to forgive," leads to another question, what is the alternative? If we do not forgive, we are following Satan; that is not a good plan!

In contrast, He who was betrayed and suffered more than any man who has ever lived is Jesus Christ. His story is an inspiration to all of us. In the height of His pain he

---

[143] Twilight's Last Gleaming, Lorimar Productions (1977)

said, "Forgive them father for they know not what they do?"[144]

None of us can claim to have a fraction of the moral stamina held by the first born of God in the flesh. As a co-creator of man with God the Father, Christ did however have one major advantage over all of us in connection with his perspective on our fellow man; He knew them. He knew them for what they were, what they are and what they can become.

He knew the soldier which nailed him to the cross as possibly the gentle soul that stood with the faithful opposing the one third of the host of heaven that rebelled against the Plan of Salvation presented by God the Father. He knew them as excited spirit sons of God, eager to enter mortality and to gain a body. The soldiers were probably on the same *jumping platform* from which they bid farewell "until they met again" as they fell into the mortal world. Christ could have remembered just enough to know for certain that truly, *they knew not what they did.*

Coming from the throne of God, they entered the world into Roman homes, pagans and idol worshipers. They were raised in a brutal and corrupt society feasting on brutality and barbarism. How could they have been expected to know of spiritual matters? Maybe they were, maybe they weren't, we don't know, nor or we expected to know. This is a matter better left to God.

As for us, we can take comfort in the fact that the whole world may be a mess. That is no reason to blow it

---

[144] Luke 23:34

up. So, I guess we need to forgive and not worry about the "how" because the alternative is unacceptable!

ROMAN GRAVEYARD

In the dawn of a crisp autumn morning, I ventured on a trail in the Turkish city of Pamukkale where the ancient city of Hierapolis was found. The 2700 meter mountainside is covered with a mineral that has earned it the name of "cotton castle" as the morning suns reflects from its apparent snow covered surface. In ancient Roman times, it was a magical place where the convergence of 17 hot springs emerged from the earth where the calcium carbonate mineral would sculpt its optical wonder.

Believing it to be therapeutic, the royalty of past would soothe their beleaguered bodies in its flowing water while the resident infirmity would go unimpeded to deliver its inevitable toll. The evidence of this eventuality was verified by the adjoining cemetery adorned with skillfully placed stones archiving the greatness of the deceased. In short, it appeared to be a place where they would come to spend their last days. Many remained, never to return.

They came to express a natural event, death. It appeared to become a game as they built monuments to themselves and their Gods. In life, they were inseparably connected to their pagan deity as they believed them to preside in their individual realm of responsibility over the elements of the earth. Surely, they felt the presence of the spirit as they submersed themselves in the pleasantly hospitable flow of life giving water as it came from the Gods of the earth to heal them.

The presentation must have been quite pleasing as the warm fluid filled every pore of their skin and the steam rose from their face to fill the expanse between them and the adjoining landscape; only a God could have created such a beautiful place. At some point they must have realized that life is inseparably connected to death and such a place as they were, were inseparably connected to the spirit.

The presence and sensation of the presence of the *spirit* which exists in the elements of the earth are shared with most every civilization known to man. They interpret and act upon these impressions in very different ways. The ancient Americans called it "the spirit that lives in all things."[145]

As I walked among the collapsed tombs, I sensed the *still small voice* chronicalizing what had taken place

---

[145] Native American folklore

here. So many lives led to this place by a desire to *believe* but knowing not the true nature of God.

The answers were truly all around them but they remained elusive as their spiritual sensitivity was obscured by the traditions of their fathers. Knowing no better, they lived, suffered and died in the same state of mind. Though the tepid water may not bring healing to the body, it should bring comfort to the soul, *"For man is spirit. The elements are eternal and spirit and element, inseparably connected, receive a fullness of joy."*[146]

It was however, blatantly obvious that this important piece of understanding was absent from their psyche. If they knew how to listen, this spirit would have impressed upon their minds the answers they were seeking. They could feel the love of the one true God and know of their place in His eternal family. The instruction may not have been with verse and text but an inner calmness to make all things seem "right."

It is a dimension beyond the obvious, the spiritual nature of the elements of which they were literally immersed. In this understanding they would know that they were not alone. Though not another soul in site, they would be surrounded by those imbedded in the elements themselves.[147] In the logical progression of this thought process, they would have known of the presence of a creator and that we are not here by chance. The supreme

---

[146] D&C 93:33
[147] ibid

spirit in all things was in fact the creator of all that we see around us.148

Scientists seek knowledge of how things work and what brought them to exist. The pursuit of "truth" is the only concern; there is no right or wrong. It is this drive that brought man's cumulative intellect to the modern age from the dark ages and is essential for future growth. However by denying any spiritual dimension to their perspective they have denied the level of intellectual growth that may bring knowledge beyond comprehension.

The rules that govern our world have natural laws. Through the interest of "critical thinking" our intellectuals question fundamental issues which may lie on the foundation of our definitions of right and wrong. This concept is only recognized as applicable when solving a problem.

Coincidently, the physical body is similar in processing stimulus regarding right and wrong; it is pleasure or pain in its various forms. If we took the time to recognize simple truths, we would realize that the spirit can tell the difference between joy and anguish. Looking at the world through my aging eyes, it is as if our modern society has lost its way just like our ancient Roman ancestors. Modern society has been away from the woods too long.

---

[148] Mos 3:9, 7:48,
<u>All Of The Answers Are In The Woods.</u> 2013, A.E.Jones

Our membership in the celestial family of God is a matter of choice, not pedigree.

MARTIN'S COVE
(A message for us all)

Sometimes it is not easy being raised in The Church of Jesus Christ of Latter day Saints and not have the "blood." The *blood* is the genetic linage that binds so many of the modern day members to the ancestors who sacrificed so much to build the church. They emigrated from all parts of the globe, overcame insurmountable odds and walked across the American Plains to the great Salt Lake Valley.

I have heard amazing stories of heroism and valor as the saints sacrificed all they had and many their lives for the light of the Gospel in their hearts. As much as my Primary instructors taught me that this was part of my heritage too, I felt *left out* when my friends spoke of their pioneer ancestry and I heard the words spoken from the pulpit in *familial* reverence.

My friends had loving and supportive parents who nurtured the gospel message in their homes, encouraged them to go on missions and to marry in the temple. Though my parents both loved me, the message and atmosphere at home was quite different. "Why was it so?" I would ask myself. "Why do I have this family and my friends have theirs?" I never considered it unfair, just a subject of curiosity. It was only much later in my life that I received the answer. As much as this heritage is a blessing to those who possess it, the blessings to those born outside the lineage is equally great.

I am sure that it was never intended, but I have always felt a little excluded when I would hear saints speak from the pulpit of their Mormon Pioneer Heritage. I would always joke with my convert friends that we were the "gentiles" of the bunch, not worthy of their company.

Of course, this attitude was inappropriate and a tribute to the youth and immaturity of the adolescent age. As I became older, I was able to filter these feelings out a bit, but it still seemed to be just a bit *annoying.*

I believe that this pioneer heritage is a great blessing to those who can trace the line there but it seemed that even if it was unintended, those professing this linage would hold it up as a badge of honor and in some cases, however rare, exercises it for the right of an election to heaven "made sure."

My parents converted to the church before I was born and raised me in the church, so as far as I was concerned, I was just like everyone else. Why was there a difference between us? Why were some better than others? Why was I not as good as my friend because his great, great grandfather did something that mine did not do?

It is funny how things can become so perfectly clear after so long over the simplest things. The concept of "heritage" was explained to me years later when I brought my wife and adult children to a historical site.

It was one summer some years ago that my family and I decided to travel west and visit a few sights that we have been wanting to see. Among them were Martin's Cove, Devils Gate and the Willy handcart site in southern Wyoming. It was in the morning of a crisp, cool and clear day that we flew to Denver, Colorado, rented a car and drove to Alcova, Wyoming.

Hours ahead of the family, I walked alone into Martin's Cove in the searing heat of the early July morning. The impact of the heat was softened by the gentle breeze of the western wind as it sifted through the leaves of the Aspen trees growing on the inward facing ridges. All was quiet as I sauntered off the path seeing no other soul there. Finding myself alone, I climbed the ridge and nestled among the trees while sitting on a rock to witness the cove in its entirety below.

It was a beautiful sight, one that could fill the soul with the impact of the stunning creations that could be witnessed. The leaves pivoted gently on their stem against the crystal blue heavens above as the pleasant breeze seemed to acknowledge my presence. As I was inventorying all that was around, I recalled all of the stories

280

of what had happened there. "How could something so horrible happen in such a beautiful place?" I asked myself.

Quick to answer my own question, I looked around this simple topographic feature to imagine how different my experience in this exact place would be with northwesterly winds driving subzero chills into the underdressed bodies of tired, sick and starving inhabitants.

At the base of the northwest wall was a small crescent shaped area where a handsome meadow was thriving in the prairie. "This is where I would set up," I thought. It seemed to be the only logical place to establish a base camp among the uneven contours that surrounded it. Supposing that there had been no major excavation in the grove since that time, I concluded that, that must have been the place where they were brought.

As I have spent countless hours in the "woods," I was sincerely trying to understand their plight based on my own troublesome experiences in hazardous conditions. It was at that moment, that the spirit shared with me a special gift. It was a sensation that I have felt only a few times in my life, and then only through the sacred will of the powers beyond the veil. I heard the desperate chatting around the camp and the cries of those suffering. A chill soared through my skin to the core of my frame and accompanied with a sensation of faith carried step by step from distant land to this place where many rose from this sacred cove to the eternities. It was curiously horrifying and exhilarating all at once.

It was a place where the pain and suffering of the mortal body was met by the celestial beings that came to sustain some and relieve others. It was a place where God Himself taught all of us a lesson that His ways and ours are different.[149] The circumstances that we believe to be horrific are where mortality meets immortality and the Lord receives us in glory[150] to His kingdom, eternal rest and rejoicing.

It is the legacy of what happened here that these faithful saints teach us in their lessons of sacrifice, faith and commitment. It was a moment in my life's experiences that I will never forget and always cherish; for only a moment, I had entered their world. As if to look through a window into the past, my vision reentered the present world with the knowledge that something extraordinary had happened.

It was at that moment that my outlook of these choice spirits forever changed. As I felt their spirit, it was as if they had never left but remained to deliver the precious message to all that would listen: Their sacrifice was not only for their direct decedents but for all of us. It was at that instant that I knew that they were my ancestors as much as they were those who could trace the genealogical line. They did what they did for me!

Never expecting to receive such a personal revelation, I silently wept in that sacred place among the trees, rocks, sky and meadow that had long since released its captors from its deadly grip. What had happened here was a message to the world that faith is more powerful than

---

[149] Clayton M. Christensen 2007, My Ways are not Your Ways
[150] Alma 14:11

all of the influence of nature or man. It is manifested in the lives of His children and dwells in the hearts of man to push the physical body beyond its natural capabilities.

With my heart full, I picked myself up and walked down into the meadow that I had observed from my perch. "How would they have arranged the tents," I imagined. I knelt down to examine the hard crusty soil and thought how hard it must have been to drive stakes into this frozen earth. Even with the blessing of the accepting spirit, I felt unworthy to be standing in their imagined footprints. "Here is where they must have stood. Here is where they must have laid, suffered and died," I thought.

As these vicarious thought processes were spinning in my mind's eye, my attention became focused on an approaching gentleman. Being a senior missionary assigned to that place, he politely inquired of my presence. Sharing my membership in the faith and expressing my deep appreciation for the opportunity to be present in that place, he placed his hand on my arm and invited me to come up the path a ways for some "guided" insight.

For the next few minutes, he and his eternal companion shared some of the more precious details of the past events referencing these dear saints. Still being embraced by the reverence of the recent experience, I intently listened as he outlined how the handcart company was found on the plains and brought to this cove for some small degree of protection from the harsh winds.

Among these details, my guide brought me to a specific spot just off the trail where the Prophet Gordon B. Hinkley had stood after acquiring rights to the property and concentrating it for its intended purpose. "This is where they are," he said. "Who," I asked. "Those who lost their lives here; this is where they were buried," he replied. "How do you know that?" I asked. He continued to explain, "When the prophet came here to visit, he was walking on this trail and he stopped here at this spot. He turned just to the north, pointed his finger to the earth below and said "They are here."

It was a special moment for me as this loving, trusting missionary looked into my heart and knew that he could confide in me this precious truth. After he spoke this message he said, "This is a sacred thing I have told you and normally do not share this but I felt inspired to do it." My heart was filled, even more than before, as I reached into bond of love that held this team together and with their God to whom they were willing to give their lives.

It was at that moment that one of my friends who accompanied my family to the grove caught up with me. He was a good hearted comrade who was often elusive to spiritual matters during that period of time. During the entire trip to that point, he was playing with his electronic companion, a newly acquired GPS (Global Positioning System). It was a "top of the line" brand with all of the latest features that could detect your exact location anywhere on the earth with forty feet accuracy through the aid of orbital satellites.

As he reached the spot where the senior missionary and I were talking next to "the place," my friend began tapping his hand held device fervently. "That is strange," he said. "All of the sudden, this thing stopped working! Ten seconds ago, I was intersecting eight differently satellites and now they are gone!" Looking into the crystal clear sky, he scratched his head to puzzle over the conundrum......but I knew why.

As precious as this spiritual message was, I would never have heard it unless I had humbly *entered their world* to seek for truth. My *spiritual ancestry* would remain along the flow chart on the family group sheet. It is now that I know, more than ever, that we are all ancestors of these great examples. All we have to do is to *enter their world* and become part of the legacy they began.

Though we cannot stand in pioneer day celebration and wave our certified pedigree, we can know that a spiritual pedigree is what the Lord recognizes. We do not need papers, credentials or passports, only the commitment to follow our faith to the ends of the earth and take whatever challenges are delivered to us by life. We only need a pure heart to land at the feet of the Savior hearing the worlds, "Well done, Thou good and faithful servant."

The credentials of a pioneer were manifested on the plains of North America in the mid nineteenth century. Today they are manifest in the lives of the people, in their hearts and in their deeds. We are not called upon to pull handcarts but our burden may be no lighter under the yoke of our responsibilities in life and the endless buffetings of a corrupt society seeking the lives of our children.

We must learn from these great saints and continue their work, push forward, never give up and always have faith that the Lords will, will be done. *"All is well, all is well.*¹⁵¹ If this is our creed, we may all declare, "Yes indeed, I have pioneer heritage!"

---

151 Come, Come, Ye Saints, William Clayton 1814-1879

SECTION 6

THINGS BECOME CLEAR
AS WE LOOK BACK
"Eternal truth"

"Life is a process of understanding."

Once we are able to "look back" and see the successes and failures in our lives, we are blessed with sound judgment as we are able to see the decisions connected to the consequences. This can only come through years of experience and accumulated wisdom. A lifetime of submersion in the doctrine of Christ we obtain an eternal prospective. In this condition we have understanding that goes beyond theory or conjecture, it is truth eternal.

Chapter 38
     Love will ultimately prevail over hate, always!

LOVE WILL ALWAYS PREVAIL OVER HATE

I first met *John* when he was a young Boy Scout. He and his dad where camping at our farm along with their troop. I was joining in the fun when John came to me saying that he had been stung by a bee and that he was very allergic. Also, he did not have the Epi pen containing the antidote and that he would probably die in a short amount of time.

Recognizing the presence of melodrama in the description of his condition, I knew that immediate attention was obviously needed. A quick search of the camp uncovered Dad and the three of us were off to the nearest emergency room where treatment was rendered.

We lost contact through the years though meeting on occasion at summer camp. While attending summer camp as a counselor in the Stake Presidency, I asked my old friend about his son John. It had been nearly ten years since that campout in the woods behind my house. "He joined the Army," he said. We spoke of family and church and renewed our friendship as we sat on the picnic table that hot summer evening.

It was a year later that the phone rang in the hall of a ward building one Wednesday evening during youth night. As chance would have it, the first counselor in the Stake Presidency was standing nearby to answer. The voice on the other end asked for a family member of John. The caller was a representative of the United States Army and was having difficulty reaching his parents to convey an urgent message.

Convincing the caller that he was an ecclesiastical representative to the family, my friend was given the tragic news and was asked to convey it to the family. John was killed in action by an improvised explosive device (IED) on the streets of Bagdad, Iraq. To say the least, the family was devastated.

A couple close to the parents came to their home within moments. The good sister held John's mom in her arms as she wept uncontrollably. The sister sang every song in the hymnal from revealed memory. Not a word was missed nor a note sung off key.

The impact of the tragedy was multiplied by several factors. John and his wife fell in love very quickly after meeting for the first time and in due course become a joyful new father. His son was born the day before John was killed. John received the news of the birth and a newborn picture on his computer the morning he was called to go out on patrol.

John's body was delivered to the Stake building in full "Class A" uniform and would receive full military honors. The wife, holding her newborn boy, was on the front row with the grieving family. The pain embroidered on their faces was distinctive. My heart was breaking as I shared in grief of that painful moment.

As the side door was opened and the three members of the presidency preceded the casket and family into the parking lot for the processional, the image was forever burned into my memory.

It was during this period of time when a very misguided religious sect was celebrating the death of soldiers as their way to protest homosexuality. As a result, an organization calling themselves the "Patriot Guard" was positioned shoulder-to-soldier on the walkway to the Hurst. They are all military veterans who rode motorcycles vowing to protect the family from any uninvited guests.

They were standing *at attention*, each with an American Flag on an eight foot staff. As the flags blew in the wind, the colors of red, white and blue filled the breeze as honor and respect was displayed in a way that only a war veteran can. Mostly veterans from the Viet Nam campaign, these fine men knew what the lack of respect was upon their return home and they were determined that this good soldier have something different.

As we walked between them, all that was heard was the sound of the flapping fabric of the flags in the breeze, the sounds of our own footsteps and the weeping of the

291

grieving widow just behind me. The traffic on the adjoining street had come to a complete stop as the occupants stood at attention by their open doors, directly in the travel lanes with their right arms being raised in a proper military salute.

It was all that I could do to keep from dropping to my knees as I heard this sweet young woman speak as she watched her husband being placed in the back of the hearse by the color guard. She said in a tender but small voice, "my sweetie." The tears were streaming from her face as she embraced her one week old boy.

With more strength than I can imagine, she turned to enter the vehicle behind us to travel the short distance to the cemetery. I was astonished as we passed lines of people on both sides of the road standing at attention. Some were in uniform, some were in suits and others were in street clothes but all were standing quietly as we passed. Fathers were standing next to their small children after obviously having coached them on how to stand and what to do. They would raise their small palms to their heads and wave to the streaming procession of motorcycles slowly roaring down the road.

The flags hanging from the bikes were seemingly endless, allowing safe and immediate passage to the graveside and assuring that the family would be insulated from whatever political agenda might await them. It seemed that the entire community had lost a member of their family as they came out to pay their respects. The display of love and concern was beyond description or even imagination. The usual ceremony ensued, the flag was

292

offered by a "Grateful Nation" and we returned to our homes with our lives being forever changed.

Besides being astounded by the display of basic goodness in the hearts of the people in the community, my capacity to understand on another level was enlarged that day. Never in my life have I witnessed such a contrast between Love and Hate as I did that day.

It was not a roadside bomb that killed John, it was Hate. It was not the insurgent that planted that device and detonated for maximum damage, it was Hate. It was not for political ideology that planted unbelievable grief and pain into the hearts of a mother, father, brother, sister and an entire community, it was Hate. It was hate that I felt was the enemy that caused the tears to fall down the beautiful face of the grieving widow as she lovingly called to her beloved companion, "sweetie."

As a society, I no longer believe we understand what the word really means. It is used too casually in our everyday language. We hate spinach, we hate that stupid television and we hate the neighbors. This is not what I felt that day; that was not the kind of hate I felt. It was abhorrence, revulsion and loathing. These are the only words we can use to describe the condition in the English language but it was something even more; it was Satanic.

What I felt was the hate associated with the desire to destroy all that is good and pure, to destroy the sons and daughters of God and to frustrate the Plan of Salvation. Its author was he who was thrown from Fathers presence for rebellion and has become the father of all lies, deception and wars. He does his dirty deeds by filling the hearts of men to spread pain, fear and darkness across the world. It went from the desolate and godless streets of Iraq to the quiet suburban streets of our Stake and into the homes of all that were associated with the event.

Their reaction was not one of hate. It was one of kindness and love. Satan is loosed to test us but he will never win. We know this. It was proven that day in the eyes of the strangers standing on the streets the sidewalks and on the front yard of their homes. It was shown by the fireman who stood at attention beneath the adjoining one hundred foot latter truck archway that covered the highway for the approaching motorcade. It was shown by more policemen I ever imagined existing in an entire state much less one community, who came out on their own time to pay respect and assist in the processional.

It was love whereby our Savior Jesus Christ stood patiently as his tormentors whipped him with fags and drove the crown of thorns into his sinless head. It was love that drove the Savior to carry his own cross through the streets of Jerusalem to Calvary where he would be murdered by evil men. It was in love that He hung there, bled, suffered and died so He could atone for our sins.

Love is greater than hate in every way. Love is the instrument of God. Hate is the instrument of Satan. Let us remember this as we are so quick to use the word in our language. Let's remember the love of the Savior to us as we preside in our families. It is through love that our church is guided. It is through love that the Prophets have given their time, talents and their entire lives for the building up of the kingdom of God.

I never want to feel the evil I felt that day again. However, the overwhelming love displayed that day by everyone I saw was a testimony to me that love will always prevail over Hate, always!

**Our Lord and Savior once walked the earth
as a perfect example.**

CHRIST

(What kind of man was He?)

It is always by example that we learn the most. We learn by doing, seeing and feeling. Every teacher knows that the kinesthetic experience is the one where the student learns by doing, hands on. Jesus Christ knows this principle all too well. It was in His example to us that we learn about what kind of people we should all be; after all, He was the only person to ever walk the earth that made no mistakes, committed neither crime nor sin.

He was (and is) the God of this world who came to take on the sins of the world and to walk among us as a mortal...having a body of flesh and bone, He was subject to pain, suffering and even temptation but having an immortal origin, He had the literal choice over life and death.

The greatest man to ever take a breath walked the streets of Jerusalem in the meridian of time. He was known as Jesus, even Jesus Christ.

With this condition of life, He had more power to influence man, nations and even the elements of the earth that any of us could imagine but with the power of the universe at His command, He choose to be our servant. Through love, patience, tenderness and compassion, He showed us the way...to live, to grow and to be happy. He willfully submitted Himself to the will of evil men so that the eternal purposes of the infinite atonement could be accomplished.

As I have contemplated the majesty of this Man, I have often wondered what it would have been like to walk with Him as the original apostles did, or maybe just as a common man who followed Him along his way to hear His messages. Obviously, there were many among Him who knew what He was. There were others who didn't. Some just followed along for the curious nature of His unexplainable personal attraction while they were accompanied by those who did so to trap Him in His words and condemn Him by the way.

Because He was a human being, He had the same physical needs as all of us did. He became hungry, sleepy and fatigued. He was a young man with a mission and He went about it with design and purpose. Having lived during those times, would we have been one of the ones who would have *known?*

Certainly, we would like to have imagined ourselves to be among His followers, but do we understand how difficult it would have been under the circumstances of the day? His best friend and senior apostle Peter, denied Him three times after declaring that it would never happen. Would we have been different?

This is an answer that only the Lord Himself could answer for us. I am sure that one day in the certain future; we will get a chance to ask. The interesting part of this discussion is to try to imagine what kind of man He was. What was He like, really?

It may seem like a simple and senseless question. The scriptures are full of the accounts of His life and His ministry. We know what kind of a man he was; he was perfect. Yes, but what was His personality? Did He have fun, indulge in jovial camaraderie among his friends? It is interesting to imagine what that part of Him would have been. Let's review some of the teachings we know of Him and see if we can gain any insight.

It was while reading the account of the Sermon on the Mount that I first imagined what it must have been like to have been there and to have heard Him. *"Blessed are the poor in spirit: for theirs is the kingdom of heaven."*[152] I would imagine that this is the first time those attending would have ever heard these words in this specific order, least of all coming from a man who spoke with such power and authority. It was not in a synagogue where these teachings are customarily reinforced with ornate marble and costly works of brass; it was on the grassy side of a hill facing the Sea of Galilee, near Capernaum. Wow, *this is*

---

[152] Matt 5:3

different, they must have imagined. He went on, *"Blessed are they who morn: for they shall be comforted."*[153] Comforted by who, what, may have been the following question but as he continued, the spirit surely fell among the most worthy among them to understand of what He was speaking.

He went on to bless the merciful, the pure in heart and the peacemakers. This being during a time of the brutal oppression of the Roman Empire, the Jewish people were surely looking for a *Savior* who could free them (the chosen people) from the tyranny, yet He was speaking of peace and making peace. *"Blessed are the peacemakers: for they shall be called the children of God."*[154]

War was known as the means to the end during those times. It was what built the Roman Empire, what conquered the Jewish Empire and what made them subject to the Roman unjust rule. It was the sword and the soldier who dictated winners and losers, yet this man spoke of peace! Where will there be the relief we have been promised if this man only speaks of peace? *"Blessed are they which are persecuted for righteousness sake: for theirs is the kingdom of Heaven."*[155] Ok, we know about kingdoms but what is a kingdom of Heaven? Furthermore, who is this man and from where does He receive His authority to testify of these things?

---

[153] Matt 5: 4
[154] Matt 5:9
[155] Matt 5:10

As His teachings fell from His gentle lips onto the meadow and rocks hosting the multitude, the countenance of a God must have fallen upon Him as the Holy Spirit manifested the divinity of the Christ, the very son of God. Isn't it true that the things manifested to the heart are infinitely more powerful than the things of the mind? As the *rushing mighty wind* [156] entered their hearts a great and unfaltering testimony of the truthfulness of His words would have certainly been followed by a peaceful and calm heart to scream from within that this is Jesus, the Savior of the world.

He taught them to pray and spoke of the treasures of heaven. He taught parables which may have pierced their souls for a desire to be better and to be more like Him.

Following that magnificent event, He sought no accolades, no applause nor any praise of man. He simply came *down from the mountain.* [157] It is said that *great multitudes followed Him* [158] for the appetite He had created could never be quenched by those seeking the comfort the Holy Spirit gives.

It tells much of a man in the way he is around little children. Jesus loved children and loved being around them. There were those among Him who felt that His time should be spent on more "important" things than with the kids, but He said, *"Suffer little children and forbid them not, to come unto me: for of such is the kingdom of*

---

[156] Acts 2:2
[157] Matt 8:1
[158] ibid

Heaven. [159] As the children ran to be close to Jesus they must have felt of His love and purity in a way that only children can. They wanted to be with Him as a friend and loving companion. As worrisome adults do, Christ's followers, who were with Him, would shoo them away as a nuisance. Being the God of this earth, He saw into their sweet hearts and pure souls and surly felt the wholesome spirit that must have greatly contrasted with those He was choosing to walk among to teach. "Please, let me rest with them for a moment and rejoice in their sweetness," would have been an understandable sentiment.

Isn't it true that so many of us take comfort and joy in the presence of the young innocence? There cannot be a more precious time in our lives when we hold a grandchild in our arms after they address us in our appointed but loving nickname, Pops, Grammy, Grannie, or Granddad. To look into their eyes is to peer into the heavens and see all that is right in the world; it gives us new hope for the future.

Our Savior was the same in this regard but with a major advantage. He *knew* them in a way not possible for us. He could see into their souls. He knew their infirmities, their talents and abilities. He knew who they were and what they could become and He loved them. His pure and perfect spirit shared the sweet condition of total innocence as they were without sin before the Lord in an age prior to accountability.

---

[159] Matt 19: 14

This point is further emphasized in a later experience with a twelve year old *damsel* described in the gospel of Mark, who appeared to be dead. As *"He cometh to the house of the ruler of the synagogue,"[160]* He addressed the damsel as Talitha Cumi.[161] A study of the ancient Hebrew language would more correctly translate this to mean, "curly hair." Addressing this young woman in this manner implies an endearment; He *knew* her even though they had never met. She "straightway...rose and walked."[162]

Can you imagine the looks in the eyes of those present? The curly haired little girl that had suddenly felt her spirit summoned from the eternities to the refreshed body that she had presently abandoned as it began its deformation process. New life had entered its arms and legs. We can only imagine what infirmities had preceded her death which was suddenly cleansed from her frame, no pain, no suffering, only joy and happiness. The first face she must have seen as her newly healed eyes reopened to the first glimmer of mortality was the glowing countenance of the savior of the world, her God and redeemer, Jesus Christ.

As she danced around the room, her parents must have fallen to their knees in astonishment and the overwhelming presence of the power and majesty of the eternal power being wielded by a God in their presence.

---

[160] Mark 5:38
[161] Hebrew translation
[162] Mark 5:42

Searching for words as their precious little curly haired girl rejoiced in life. With the power to defeat death and the manifestation of this authority the Lord Jesus sought no aggrandizement but, *"charged straitly that no man should know it."*[163] Does this sound like a man that would deliberately bring attention to Himself? His actions of charity and benevolence were for the benefit to others, never for the praise of man. This is the kind of man He was!

In studying the Bible, I am impressed with His mastery of the language. He could express His feelings in such a unique and interesting way without being offensive. For example, in Luke, Jesus was warned by a certain Pharisee, *"Get thee out, and depart hence; for Herod will kill thee."*[164] In an obvious expression of confidant defiance, He replied, *"Go ye, and tell that fox, Behold, I cast out devils, and I do cures today and tomorrow, and the third day I shall be perfected."*[165] Now, it is interesting here to remember that Jesus knew Herod more than any man; He *created* his body as it came from our first parents Adam and Eve. He knew what he was. Jesus also knew what His mission here on earth was and that nothing, no power or dominion on earth would frustrate His appointed goal.

Jesus also created the animals of the earth. He knew the fox and what it was created to do. A fox is a predator, a carnivore and was created this way by design. It fulfills its

---

[163] St Mark 5:43
[164] Luke 13:31
[165] Luke 13:32

purpose in the fabric of natural things. It is known for its cunning nature and for its ability for stealth when necessary.

For Jesus to call Herod a fox is interesting, isn't it? It is not an insult; He simply identifies Herod for what he is, a cunning predator of the earth whose purpose is to strike in silence for its selfish personal appetite. A fox has no conscious, no moral character or benevolence; it is a fox and so was Herod.

With all of the miracles Jesus preformed and with all of the good He did throughout the land, His desire was to draw attention to His father and not to himself. The proof of this can be determined by a careful linking of several scriptures in the Gospel of John, *"Then answered Jesus and said unto them, verily, verily, I say unto you, the son can do nothing of himself, but what the seeth the father do for what things soever he doeth these also doeth the son likewise."*[166]

Now, couple this with verse 30, *"I can of mine own self do nothing: as I hear, I judge: and my judgment is just; because I seek not mine own will, but the will of the Father which hath sent me."* The succession of thought continues in verse 16 of Chapter 7, *"Jesus answered them and said, My doctrine is not mine but his that sent me."* As if this is not enough to drive home the point, Jesus states the same principle another way in Chapter 8 verse 28... *"I do nothing of myself; but as my Father hath taught me I speak these things."*

---

[166] John 5:19

Christ's greatest example to us was one of obedience. He does nothing *for himself* but only seeks to please His father, *"and he that sent me is with me: the Father hath not left me alone for I do always those things that please Him."*[167] What kind of friend would He be to us? As we follow Him around the countryside, He does these wonderful and amazing things but says *it is not of me!*

This attribute seems contrary to the ways of men and the world...and that is the point. He, Jesus, was not of this world, but was the very Son of God. He knew it and could never be off course from His eternal goals and purposes.

It is often in the simple examples that we can learn great things. For example, at the door of Lazarus' tomb, Jesus said, *"Take ye away the stone."*[168] One might ask the question, why would Jesus ask that the stone be taken away? If He was going to raise someone *from the dead* why couldn't He have just pointed His mighty finger and levitate the door up a story or two and have it fly across the street for a while? There may be many correct answers for this question but I would submit that from the lessons we learn from studying His life and His personality, His exercising of His great power was only what was necessary to accomplish the goal. He would never use the power given Him by the Father for any unnecessary task, no matter how insignificant it may seem.

---

[167] John 5:29
[168] St. John 11:39

With all that He had done and said, after all of the miracles, countless sermons where the angles of truth were present and the love and sacrifice He had given among the children of men, He was rejected by his own. This must have been his sentiment as He sat on the Mount of Olives and said the words that we have come to know so intimately, *"O Jerusalem, Jerusalem, thou that killest the prophets, and stonest them which are sent unto thee, how often would I have gathered thy children together, even as a hen gathereth her chickens under her wings, and ye would not."*[169] Nearing the end of His ministry, the Savior expressed a sentiment of frustration as He looked upon the city that would seal His eternal fate ending in His crucifixion and resurrection.

He knew his mission, goal and destiny and He fulfilled it faithfully and completely. He cries for the father to *"forgive them as they know not what they do."*[170] Having iron nails driven into His feet and hands, hanging from a cross made from a tree and vertically posted to perish in ultimate agony, He still seeks for mercy for those taking his mortal life. Surely, we would join with John in asking the question, *"what kind of man is this…that even the winds and sea obey him."* [171]

We should all be able to answer this question by now, what kind of man is this? He is the Son of God, He is the God of this world, He is the Savior and redeemer of

---

[169] Matt 23:37

[170] Luke 23:34

[171] Matt 8:27

every man that has ever, is or will walk on the earth. He joined with the Father to create man for His eternal purposes and has joy in our joy. He wants us to follow Him as He follows His father. He is our ultimate example and perfect mentor. By seeking Him, we will find happiness and joy. His attributes are Faith, Hope, love and Charity. This is who Jesus is; a very true friend!

**The Lord's name should always
be spoken in reverence.**

IN HIS HOLY NAME

In the lifetime of any boy growing to manhood in The
Church of Jesus Christ of Latter-Day Saints, it is certain
that he has heard and repeated the sacred name of Jesus
Christ a countless times. Hopefully, it was always heard or
spoken in reverence. In all that we do and say to further His
kingdom, His name is repeated many times. We dedicate
meetings to Him, bless every meal in His name and
supplicate His blessings several times a day in personal,
spousal and family prayers. We plead for guidance in our
daily efforts, appeal for good will for those in need of
comfort and seek His counsel as we go about His work in
the kingdom. His name is prominently displayed on our
places of worship and on His Temples. He is our purpose,
our goal and our ambition. *"We talk of Christ, we rejoice*

in Christ, we preach of Christ, we prophesy of Christ"[172] His name and His legacy are sacred to us as we pursue our life's ambitions and interact with our fellow man.

Being raised in the South, I have regularly heard people of "faith" call upon His name with aggressive casualness. With no apparent respect for the majesty of the Being they are hailing, they raise their voice and elongate the consonants in a stream of wailing as if to summon a beast from the field. In the process, they implore the praise of men as they make a spectacle for the benefit of all in attendance.

Many are taken with the excitement and theater of the flamboyant process and are taught to believe that what they are feeling is spiritual and inspirational. Their personal supplications for spiritual experiences are substituted with "flash and fanfare" that teaches one hundred truths with every falsehood.

In all of this teaching I have heard from every good natured believer I have befriended in my life, I have often considered what they would do if they ever really knew the nature and majesty of the Savior Jesus Christ. The testimony of Joseph Smith rang so true with me as he recalled the words spoken to him in the sacred grove, *"They draw near to me with their lips but their hearts are far from me, they teach for doctrines the commandments of men, having a form of godliness, but they deny the power thereof."[173]* Certainly this is evident today.

---

[172] 2 Nephi 25:26
[173] JSH 1:19

How different would their boisterous public summoning be if they knew the powers they were calling upon?

In my advancing years, I believed that over a lifetime of experience in the Kingdom, I understood the nature of God as well as I could. It was not until a voyage beyond my southern comfort zone that I became exposed in a small way to how wrong I was.

My wife and I took the opportunity to journey to the Promised Land some years ago to the city of Jerusalem. "What an honor," I thought, to be in the land where The Christ lived in mortality. I would imagine that He walked on the same streets I walked and perhaps rested on this same path side as I did. I could feel his presence so intensely as I passed under the overpass where Pilot supposedly threw down the verdict to condemn our God.

We went to the pit below Calopious' house where the Savior was imprisoned while false witnesses were assembled. We walked the trail to Golgotha as I imagined those assembled to mock and ridicule our Lord and Savior.

There were those who assembled themselves at the place where some claim He was crucified, inside the city walls. There was an open display of wailing and mourning as the tourist pushed and shoved their way in line to obtain their own "spiritual experience." The reported burial tomb was conveniently located below the point of crucifixion where you were forced to kneel below the protruding metal bars forcing you to your knees.

As I looked upon the panorama, I was quietly disturbed over the ostentatious ornamentation surrounding the scene as if to demand reverence under such a display of wealth and worldly majesty. Without understanding the intended purpose, you could surmise, "It must be true. Look at all that gold and silver!"

Those who follow the "philosophies of man mingled with scripture" have come to feel that the powers that created them as one of cold omnipotence demanding His creations to worship Him. In contrast to what I expected, what I felt among the crowd was not peace but deception: Surely, this is not what He would want.

The subtle but powerful delivery of the spirit did have great impact on me however, in another place. The group we were traveling with comprised a half dozen LDS couples and we sat on the Mount of Olives to study the scriptures and contemplate the events of the past. It was a quiet time, a peaceful time. There was no grieving crowds or vocal outcry of praise. There was only us.

I gathered myself on top of a stone wall overlooking the eastern gate of Jerusalem where Christ entered for the last time. It is covered over now with stone and fronted with a grave yard as if to "dare" His triumphant return. The words of the Gospels were gently filling the gentle breeze as I pondered where the Lord was sitting where He recited the words, *"Oh Jerusalem, Jerusalem, how often I would have gathered you under my wings but you would not."*[174] It was near this spot that He offered the prayer of supplication to His Father, *"Take this cup,"*[175] and then

---

[174] Matt 23:37
[175] Matt 26:42

accepted the cup where He bled from every pore of His precious body.[176]

Following the Atonement, the greatest event in the history of all mankind, He was betrayed by Judas and delivered into the hands of evil men who would deliver perhaps the most agonizing and brutal death ever devised by men.

Beyond the modern turmoil that perpetuates to this day among the descendants of those ancient inhabitants, the place is quiet and still. I looked up to the clear blue sky and inhaled the aroma of the grove and imagined how the Savior must have loved this place of peace and beauty.

The large aged olive trees were gnarly with the effects of the years. Although I knew that none of them were probably present during His time, I imagined how they must have glowed in the countenance of the Creator of the earth when they heard His voice,

And the Gods organized the earth to bring forth grass from its own seed, and the herb to bring forth herb from its own seed yielding seed after his kind; and the earth to bring forth the tree from its own seed yielding fruit, whose seed could only bring forth the same in itself, after his kind; and the Gods saw that they were obeyed.[177]

---

[176] Mosiah 3:7

[177] Abr 4:12

This "voice" that they first heard and obeyed was now manifested in the flesh and kneeling before them addressing the heavens. The splendor and magnificence of the moment must have filled the measure of their creation as they witnessed their essential role in the fulfillment of the promise to the children of God the Father.

In the process of being tried and tested, there must be a garden both literal and figurative; tonight the only begotten Son of God the Father was here among the olive trees to accept the consequence for the sins of all men that had, are or will ever occupy the third planet from the Sun.

Falling out of my self-induced spell, I recognized the voice of our tour guide inviting me to be the voice in consecrating a vial of olive oil that had been harvested from these very trees there in Gethsemane. "Of course," I said. "It would be an honor!" With that, I hopped down from the wall and gathered in a circle of Melchizedek Priesthood holders with one hand from each brother on the open vial of oil and the other on the shoulder of the brother to our left.

Reciting the sacred words, the familiar sentences were vocalized the same as a thousand times before as I consecrated the oil for the healing of the sick, and I closed, as customary, in the holy and sacred name of Jesus Christ.

It was at that moment that the impact of His holy name shot through me as a lightning bolt from the two millennia past declaring that HE LIVES. Though the men who led Him to His mortal parting supposed victory that evening, the majesty, power and eternal realm of the God on earth, reigns supreme to every puny power ever assembled by the self-proclaimed superpowers on earth. "In the Sacred name of Jesus Christ" echoed from the stone eastern walls of the city like a shock wave of a passing sonic blast declaring to the world that Jesus is the Christ, He lives, He has conquered death and reigns as the eternal God to all on Earth. His splendor, magnificence, elegance and power are beyond imagination and we all would shrivel in His presence.[178]

Knowing this, would any call His name for the sake of personal gain? Understanding the true power of God embodies reverence, love and respect. His name is honored, revered and cherished. We fall to our knees as we consider His approach and precious presence.

I have often been asked what I would ask of the Savior if given the chance. In consideration of this question I do not know that I could ask anything. I do not believe I would have the courage to remove myself from the floor much less look up into His precious eyes.

The impression at the grove was not one of condemnation or unworthiness however, though I thought it would be. It was a feeling of "home," a place where I was welcome no matter my infantile state. I have always known that He loved me. This experience confirmed it. He loves all of His family. We are all family, together.

As I left the circle following consecrating the oil, I quietly walked behind the olive trees in the near distance and wept from the weight of the presence of His Spirit and the magnitude of the immediate events. As I contemplated

---

[178] JST Exodus 33:20

my insignificance in the presence of the righteousness men on earth, I figuratively felt the calming presence of the same Jesus Christ from old seem to lay His gentle hands upon my shoulder as if to provide comfort in His presence.

It is imperative that we all take the time to consider our relationship with our Savior and how we honor His name and memory. The next time we repeat the words, consider if we really understand what it means when we say, "In His Holy name, even Jesus Christ, amen."

KINDNESS
(God's gift to Man)

Since I was a boy, I always imagined myself as a soldier. It was a boyhood fantasy more than an ambition. However, as I grew into young adulthood and reviewed my options, I decided to pursue it as a career. I felt it an honor to serve the country that I loved and counted myself proud to be among those who have worn the uniform.

I remember during training, listening to the instruction and realizing that I was using all of the intellect within me to acquire knowledge to most effectively *neutralize* a threat (take the life of an enemy). It was an *academic exercise*. In field artillery, what type of round should be placed where to affect the maximum benefit: damage. At some point I realized that the lesson was actually how to keep America safe from those who would harm her.

During the conflict described in the Book of Mormon, Captain Moroni had no desire for violence: he wanted peace. He realized that the only way to have peace was to defeat those who would cause harm to their *"faith, religion and their rites of worship."*[179] As violence is the tool of darkness, it must be met with violence in order to *neutralize* those who choose to do evil.

The pattern of violence both on the offensive and defensive are the blueprint of human existence and will continue to be so long as there are evil ambitions in the hearts of man. Obviously, violence is not a desirable attribute for the children of God.

Following my military experience, there were many years of difficult adjustment into the civilian world. I never felt that I ever "came home." Once the spirit of war enters your heart, it is difficult (if not impossible) to ever remove it. I was puzzled over the glamour associated with conflict by those who would profit from it in the realm of entertainment.

Countless hours are spent in simulated war games by our youth yielding weapons of war to "neutralize" an imaginary enemy complete with graphic displays of blood and dismemberment. Awards and accolades are granted those who can kill the most enemies in the least amount of time over the widest area of engagement. In the process, the amount of violence desensitizes the player to seeing it

---

[179] Alma 44:5

as only an *academic exercise*. However, at some the academic exercise becomes all too real and he may never be able to distinguish the difference and forever be haunted by the spiritual and psychological implications.

I remember sitting on the front row waiting to pass the Sacrament as a young deacon. My testimony was emerging from obscurity as I felt the spirit of that holy ordinance. I could feel the presence of the Holy Ghost as I exercised my priesthood and fulfilled my callings in the church. There was a spirit of love, joy and kindness associated with the work and toward my brothers and sisters in the Kingdom. There was a peace there that I longed for later as I held the assault rifle in my hands realizing what I must do to keep my country free. Of all the training my fellow soldiers and I received, *kindness* was not among the disciplines studied.

It would appear that war is the result of a total breakdown in, "the practice of being or the tendency to be sympathetic and compassionate."[180] In the act of giving and receiving kindness; happiness, love and joy accompany the experience.

However, time and time again over the millennia of human existence, the absence of kindness has led to conflict, bloodshed and war. War is as far from kindness as anyone can imagine. By definition, it represents hostility, conflict, struggle and the embodiment of pain and suffering.

---

[180] Encarta Dictionary: kindness

Through a simple analysis of these opposing conditions it would appear a simple conclusion that kindness is good and violence is bad. To further that deductive reasoning, it would appear logical that kindness is the tool of God and violence and war is the tool of Satan.

With this simple hypothesis, we can advance our logic: where there is kindness there is joy and where there is joy there is God. Kindness therefore is a gift from God Himself for us to use in this life filled with choices.

"And this is the manner after which they were ordained—being called and prepared from the foundation of the world according to the foreknowledge of God, on account of their exceeding faith and good works; in the first place being left to choose good or evil."[181] It is difficult to believe why anyone would choose evil, yet we see it every day on the streets, in the news and perhaps, in our own lives. It persists in the hearts and minds of the world and we cannot help but be in some way involved.

Those among us who have lived surrounded by the spirit of contention, long for the peace that accompanies kindness. The events of kindness fill the recorded life of the Savior as He healed the sick, made the lame walk and held the sweet faces of the children in His hands. He taught with love and compassion to "follow Him" as He walked perfectly in the light that leads to the celestial world. The peace of His kindness calms our hearts as we discover that as we exercise kindness, our capacity to show it grows.

---

[181] Alma 13:3

Even in the world today, this condition exists amongst the jungle of strife. It is present in its fullness as embodied in the restored gospel of Jesus Christ. The condition of kindness, love and joy lives in the homes of loving parents who support and guide their children to follow Him in all that they do and say. It lives in the hearts of loving and supportive church leaders who sacrifice their time, talents and all that the Father has given them to build up the kingdom of God. It lives in the thousands of missionaries that serve across the globe to bring a message of salvation and exaltation to all those willing to listen.

Kindness is the act of compassion that reaches out to those who have strayed from the straight and narrow path with the gentle correction, "come follow me." It is selfless and self-sacrificing for the benefit of others without recognition save it be for the Master Himself. Kindness is a condition of eternal life and the ultimate source of the atonement of Jesus Christ.

In every act of the mortal ministry of the Savior we see kindness. As we follow His admonition, *"Be even as I,"*[182] should we not follow suit? Kindness is a gift from our Father in Heaven that allows us to be like Him. As a result, we become closer to Him by following in His footsteps and becoming more like Him.

Kindness is a simple thing, really. As a boy, it was my job to cut the grass of our rural home. It was about two acres that I cut with a large rear wheel 18" wide gas mower. As you can imagine, it was a long arduous process.

---

[182] 3 Nephi 28:10

I don't remember why, but I do remember that on one occasion our neighbor came over with a tractor that had a 72" belly mower. Without hesitation (or effort) he reduced the job to a moment with a soda pop and a smile on his face. I stood to the side and watched in awe as the large machine effortlessly completed my weekly task in mere moments. I felt as though every footstep and struggle to push the heavy mower over the tall grass was being removed from my extremities and joy filled my heart.

He did not have to do it, but he did. It was a simple act of kindness that has fondly touched my memory some fifty years later. It is a goal that we should all strive for as we understand that it is the reflection of an eternal principle that, kindness, is God's gift to man.

Truth, Eternal #: 42
        Death is nothing to fear.

OH DEATH,
WHERE IS THY STING?

(A Sound Understanding)

I was a twelve year old Deacon when I first remember facing the death of a friend. Death seemed so far away, something experienced by "old" people and not something I needed to be concerned with.

He was the younger brother of one of my friends. Only last weekend we had been playing games in his neighborhood swimming pool throwing water balls and playing *Marco-polo*.

My Mom had received a phone call from a Sister in the Ward announcing the tragic news that he was killed in a car accident yesterday, "But I saw him last Saturday," I said. "They would like you to be a Pall Bearer," she replied. I hung my head as I considered what all of that meant. "How could this be?" I thought.

As the following weekend approached, a few of my friends and I set on the same front row where we wait to pass the sacrament. The Casket was just in front of us holding the remains of our mutual friend. I listened to the adults as they talked about my friend and the circumstances of the tragic event. Tears laced the outpouring of the doctrine as his Dad spoke for his love for his son and his faith that he was in Heaven with his Eternal Father.

Eight of us struggled under the enormous weight of the coffin as we carefully carried it to the graveside. It seemed so heavy that I thought I would have to use both hands to hold it up but they told me that I had to use only one. Although my faith was tender, I knew that what they said was true. I wondered why he was taken before he had a chance to grow up. Although these were the impressions to a boy, similar thoughts persist in all of us as adults.

We have all developed acquaintances in our lives; it is unavoidable. In some cases, we share ideas, ideals and values with a few that become friends. We enjoy the exchange of thoughts and dreams. We have common interests in activities, hobbies or passions. Among these friends, we develop a pattern of association that evolves into an enduring relationship. These friends become our adoptive family in every sense of the word. The members of our *family* represent an "inner circle" of relationship that is very close to our emotional world. This personal emotional world, inhabited by our family, travels the paths

323

of life along our side and has a deep impact on our own human condition.

We travel the path together looking out for each other along the way. We depend on each other and help when one struggles, stumbles or falls. This is what friends do, right?

We expect them to always be there, just like they have always been. These are those friends who always cheerfully accept our phone calls regardless of the time or topic. We can drop by any time and they are always happy to see us and anxious to be caught up on the current topics. These relationships can become particularly close when we share the inner most feelings of spirit and testimony relating to the Gospel of Jesus Christ and the restored eternal truths.

There have been many through the years that I have called "Brother." This is an *inner circle* of those I would choose to share in life's experiences and challenges. These are those who have gained my respect and admiration through their commitment to their values, faith and family. I sought their company because they helped to make me a better person and represented the good things I sought in my life. It was not until later in life that I experienced the loss of one so close and felt the impact of the event and the effect it would have on my life.

I was sitting in my office one work day when an associate walked in and said, "Andy, You need to go and check on your friend Pat. He was taken to the emergency room this morning and is in pretty bad shape." Within that same moment, I took my leave.

Pat was one of *those guys,* a good and faithful servant who loved the Lord and his family. He was strong in every way and gifted in many extraordinary ways. Pat would always have the answers to every question I would have over an apparent infinite array of subjects relating to electrical, mechanical or industrial issues. I would call him the "Font of all knowledge" as he would humbly laugh in reproach. We spent many nights by the campfire sharing stories relating to our callings and challenges with kids and jobs…I loved this man.

I approached the reception desk in the expansive foyer of the hospital and inquired as to his room assignment. Several hours had passed between the time the incident had occurred and my receiving the information, I figured he had been assigned a room by now. Knowing that his unique last name could not be confused with another, I was puzzled when they could not find him in the directory. Refusing to believe my information to be inaccurate, I walked around to the Emergency room entrance where I saw his wife emerging from the inner door with the obviously shaken Stake President at her side.

Observing the expression of his face, I feared the worse. Refusing to accept this impression, I approached her and asked, "Where is my friend?" In response to my simple question, Pats loving and faithful wife looked up at me and simply and calmly said, "He has gone to live with his Heavenly Father." In her eyes, there was no fear, contention or doubt. It was only minutes before that his condition was declared but she expressed his present status as if Pat had left for an extended business trip.

Pretending comparative strength, I turned to exit the building where I began to weep in privacy. Though times of grieving would surely follow, Pat's wife had a *clear understanding* of what had happened and where her eternal companion was.

Brother Hank was a genuine Polynesian. The blood of the royal Polynesian linage flowed through his veins and his endless compassion and love for man was the basis for all that he did. He earned the love and respect of many, including myself. I loved this man. Hank was my *Brother*.

As he was diagnosed with Colin cancer, I refused to believe that it would make any change in Hank's endless life as he continued to bless others. I would later accompany him to the sessions of chemo therapy as the nurses would smile and welcome him for treatment. He made them feel special along with all that he knew. We would joke about the "plumbing" connection on his chest that attached to the machine that would deliver treatment to his deteriorating body.

With the progressive onslaught of relentless physical blows, Hank eventually lost his capacity to resist and surrendered to the eternal world. His sweet wife asked me to accompany their youngest son to the airport to pick up their two oldest children from Brigham Young University in Provo. They approached us with cheerful hearts and joyful countenances. They were laughing and joking with each other as we retrieved their luggage and we walked to the vehicle. They were sharing stories of college, dorms and life on campus with their younger brother who joyfully joined in the conversation. I quietly listened as I drove through the late night to their home and their anxious mother.

They were Hank's children. Certainly they loved him more than I, but still, they were cheerful. As I contemplated the situation, I realized, *"They have a clear understanding!"* They know what happened to their Dad. They knew where he was and what he was doing. There was no doubt what kind of man he was and what awaited him on the other side of mortality. I thought at that moment that I needed to take a lesson from them and place my understanding in my disposition.

Bruce knocked on the door to where we were having our Stake Presidency meeting one Wednesday evening. In unison, we all stood to gleefully welcome his unexpected arrival. Sporting a "to-go" box of deep-fried hush puppies, he said, "I have an announcement to make!" Knowing that Bruce had been diagnosed with terminal pancreatic cancer several months earlier, I was anxious to hear the presumed *good news.* "I went to the doctor today, and he said that the treatment is having no effect on the cancer and has given me two months!" Though the news cut to my heart, I could only grasp for humor as I witnessed the cheerful outlook and glow in his countenance. "Do you know what that means Bruce?" I said. "You can eat all of these deep fried hush puppies all by yourself and not worry about it. Further, we should go out and get a box of glazed and jelly filled donuts and eat them all ourselves." With similar accolades, the Presidency shared in the levity as we honored this cherished son of God. He is and always has been a stalwart to the faith and the Kingdom. I loved this man. It was at that moment I realized, He has *a sound understanding!*

Death has very different meanings to most people. For the most part they refuse to think about it but they all accept it as an inevitable fact. To some, it is the end of existence. To others, it is a change of status.

As members of the Church of Jesus Christ of Latter Day Saints, we recognize death as a passing from mortality to immortality, where the spirit is temporarily separated from the body. We know that in time, the body and spirit will be reunited,

> *"The soul shall be restored to the body, and the body to the soul; yea, and every limb and joint shall be restored to its body; yea, even a hair of the head shall not be lost; but all things shall be restored to their proper and perfect frame."*[183]

Our loved ones who have traveled to the other side are in a state of peace and happiness; it is those of us who are left behind who are left alone and without their happy fellowship. Though we have this same *understanding*, we are not yet called upon to implement its truthfulness in our lives. We accept it as that which is the responsibility of those "who have been called" and it does not include us, at least not yet!

---

[183] Alma 40:23

I believe that it was in that welcome diversionary moment in our Presidency meeting that we all joined in that understanding. We laughed with Bruce and spoke of senseless dietary rebellion in defiance of the inevitable mortal ending….we understood. However, it will make the accepting of his eventuality no easier to accept because, we loved this man.

Our Father in Heaven gave His son Jesus Christ to evil men of the world who would take His life in a brutal, evil way but He allowed it to happen because he had *a clear understanding*. It is in this understanding that we find peace, joy and happiness.

My young friend's parents had it, Pat's sweet wife had it, Hank's family had it and Bruce had it. It is the least that we can do to follow in their example and implement the sound understanding we have of the plan of salvation in our lives. We should not wait until we receive the calling of death to place its principles in our lives. We should do it as if every day is our last by following the example of my friend Hank. He loved his fellow man and they knew it.
His life was his legacy and so should ours be.

As we come to embrace the restored gospel of Jesus Christ, we will all have a clear understanding that will serve us well in the walk of life both mortal and immortal. Let's live our lives where others cannot tell the difference and always maintain a *sound understanding*.

THE PASSING

How many times had I been in this place, enjoying the feeling of the wind against my skin and the warmth of the sunshine on my face? It was the small hill, deep behind the old homestead. Although the home was long since demolished, I remembered as a child retreating to this quiet place for peace and solace beneath the aged red oak tree forest. Countless layers of deciduous leaves had fallen, to begin the enrichment of the soil for another cycle of life. It was always curious to me however, that among all the falling leaves, there was a place where the green moss would grow to provide a pleasing blanket to the earth.

I loved it here. I believed that beautiful moss covering to be like a red (green) carpet, welcoming me. As I sat, recalling the reality of the day and its circumstances, I realized that much time has passed since those days. I grew

330

into a man and began my own family, rarely returning. My parents parted with much contention and went their different ways when I was still young. The property was divided and my father built a modest home adjoining this precious spot, still covered with the moss of my memories. The house was surrendering to the mold, rust and decay of its own aged condition.

Sitting on his living room sofa, I could look down upon *my* mossy hill just there in the back yard. Having remained single in the four decades following the divorce, my father was faithful to his home and garden. His wood burning stove was fed by wood that he split himself – up until a few years ago when his joints began to rebel against ninety one years of unrelenting service. He had become quite weak over the past year, falling to his knees often as his balance failed him.

At the kitchen table that morning, he poured his bowl of cereal as he prepared for fellowship during his daily trip to the senior center. The untouched cereal was still on the table above him, as his lifeless body was respectfully placed on the floor by the county coroner. The authorities departed, and my sister and I waited for the funeral home representatives to prepare Dad for the ceremonies to come. His silver gray hair had fallen in his face; he was still and quite, different that I had ever remembered. His time on earth was finished. His test was over and his days of probation were complete.

As I looked outside through the dirty glass door onto that precious mossy hill, I wondered what was different. Do the trees, hills and birds living just outside know that the spirit that resided here for so long was no longer among them? Would anything within their world be different? Of course, I knew the answer was no, at least no change that we would notice. However, in my world and in the worlds of my sisters and those who knew him, life would forever be different. It would be a life without the presence of Earl Jones. This would have its effect in varying degrees on different people. I would be left with the memory of "how things were" and what they "could have been."

I was impressed with an acute awareness of the passing of time and its purpose in our lives. For nearly 34,000 days, my dad had a chance to be what he was, what he became and what he could have been. It is the same for all of us. The house he occupied may eventually rot to the ground, the lands cleared and perhaps return to its original state of large red oaks and a mossy hill, as if the "reset button" on the game of life had been pressed.

I wonder, how many times this scene has been played across the world? How many times has a life, so long lived had such an impact on an individual, family or society, be reduced to a memory or an etching on the hillside of the earth? Following the near century of life or the millennia of a civilization, the earth is inevitably cleanses its evidence of existence to a crusting foundation of a presence long passed broken shards of pottery.

Only the soul whom has passed and the Lord Himself knows exactly what once happened there and the effects it will have on humanity. The earth however, and the mossy hill returns to its natural state giving no lasting testament of the mortal ordeal that took place on this soil: it has served its purpose as the proving ground of the sons and daughters of God.

Isn't all the earth the same? Every hill, dale and plain was created by the God of all mankind for the purpose of providing an environment in which we are to be tested. It is here that we have the opportunity to prove[184] who we are and to whom we owe our allegiance. God gives us His most precious processions, his daughters and sons to love or use, to help or to deceive or to bless or to harm.

I guess it is because of my acute sensibilities regarding elements of the earth, that I see people in their most basic elements. The statement made by the Lord, *"For dust thou wast, and unto dust shall thou return"*[185] describes our bodies as literal elements of the earth. If dust is interpreted as *dirt* then all of us are clay, sand or silt with some biological sediment thrown in. We live in houses made of wood (trees), brick (clay) and stone (sedimentary, metamorphic or igneous).

We adorn our bodies with clothing made of cotton (grown on a farm), silk (which comes from worms) or wool (which is sheared from the hides of sheep). We drive around in automobiles which are made from metal (ore from the earth), rubber (extract from trees) and leather (tanned from the hides of cattle).

---

[184] Abr 3:25
[185] Moses 4:25

Where in this understanding of what we are gives us any pride to believe we have any control over our existence or our future placement in existence? We are products of the earth "For dust thou wast, and unto dust shall thou return." In this statement, the Lord has explained clearly that we are totally in His control and live under His direction. *"And the Lord God formed man of the dust of the ground, and breathed into his nostrils the breath of life: and man became a living soul."*[186]

Of ourselves, we are nothing, we can become nothing nor could we exist. He has placed us here to test and to try us. In some places it is next to a mossy hill and in others it is surrounded in concrete and steel. It is in the deserts or on the plains. It is in the jungles or on the mountain tops. In whatever place it is, it is earth and will be returned to its paradisiacal[187] glory once its purpose is completed.

It is in this understanding that we should all gain humility knowing that our environment is the mortal stage created by the Master so we can act in all the days we are allowed to prove who we are, who we want to become and who we have the potential to be. We are given the ability to interact with others to determine if we will be a detriment or beneficial to their performance in this play which has no script or predetermined plot.

We write the script as we go and carry it with us to the mossy hill at the end of our lives to be read by the

---

[186] Gen 2:7
[187] AOF 10

creator of the earth and its surrounding universe for the audience of the heavens to hear.

Though my days of probation continue to grant me sunrises and sunsets, I will forever be on that couch during that warm sunny day on the mossy hill. I will wonder what I could do to better prepare for the day when my son approaches my still body to gently pull back the gray hair, or to glance in disinterest. Regardless of the circumstance, I only hope that as I move from this existence to the next, there will be many mossy hills to roam in the celestial forests of the eternities. Knowing that I did all that I could to reach the potential the Lord planned for me in this mortal realm we call earth.

Parting words

The story of my life would attract the interest on no one seeking excitement, intrigue or even success. Like most others, I have struggled for the means necessary to provide for my family. In this pursuit, I have faced the challenges of most to include trials and failures. Among all of the turmoil of life there has always been one thing that I have held on to. There is only one principle that is constant, unmovable and unchangeable. It is one that can always be relied upon and will never disappoint or betray, it is the Gospel of Jesus Christ.

As I sit on the pews on Sunday morning, I look around and see friends from all walks of life taking time away from their worldly lives to pay respect to their faith. It is a time of consecration when they put aside the ways of the world to reach for higher ideals afforded by the restored Gospel of Jesus Christ. It is beautiful.

The precious souls of the little children are trustingly following their parents' example as they struggle to remain reverent awaiting the excitement of Primary. They are being taught that there is more to the world than what they can see and touch. The things you can feel go beyond the physical abilities, they are feelings touch the soul.

The soul is the inner core of our beings. It is the intelligence that came from the throne of God to a world of air, dirt and sea. Our bodies can only survive it for so long and they return to the earth. *Then shall the dust return to the earth as it was: and the spirit shall return unto God who gave it.* [188]

With this being an undeniable reality to us all, it has always been a mystery to me how so many of the earth's inhabitants cling to their earthly processions as if they will never dwindle. Why else would they never seek knowledge or possessions "not of this world?"

There is certainly no crime in being wealthy. Many have used their wealth for great and noble purposes. It is those who understand that the wealth of the world should be used for the benefit of their fellow man who truly understand what it means to build up their treasure in heaven. *"Jesus said unto him, If thou wilt be perfect, go and sell that thou hast l and give to the poor, and thou shall have treasure in heaven"...* [189]

With an understanding of the Gospel comes a love of the Savior Jesus Christ and the atoning sacrifice He made for all of us. It is an understanding that survives mortality and is our lifeline to the eternities. It is the celestial sub-audible signal that connects our souls to our home of our past. It is the spirit that dwells beneath the tabernacle of clay that longs for the light and presence of our perfect Father and His perfect example. It is the entity that screams within us at the horrors of the world and its wickedness, in spite of the truth that dwells deep within them which silently cries, "there is more to life than this,

---

[188] Ecc 12:7
[189] Mark 10:21

you are a child of God, hang on, endure, prevail and all will be made right."

It is this knowledge that drives those in tune onward. It is this concept that captures their heart to declare *... ye are from beneath; I am from above: ye are of this world; I am not of this world.*[190] Sometimes, proclaiming our separation from the world is the only way to endure its burdens. We stand as a symbol for all that is good and right and defy the world to take away what we are, knowing it to be impossible. Though they may take away our lives, they cannot take our souls. One belongs to the earth, the other to He who sent us, God the Father.

He is our father, our master, director and purpose. It is His world we seek, His world we pursue and His world that we superimpose on this filthy earthly surface to the extent of our capabilities. With this mindset, there is no room for material substance beyond our needs and that to help others. In this directive that we drive forward, *But Lay up for yourselves treasures in heaven, where neither moth nor rust doth corrupt and where thieves do not break through nor steal.*[191]

Sadly, I have witnessed those of great wealth and power (as so they presume) believe that they "have it all" when in fact they have nothing. It is a sad life that hinges on their possessions. Their importance and stature in the world is a direct reflection of the balance displayed on their

---

[190] John 8:23
[191] Mat 6:20

personal financial statement. This is a pitiful measurement of happiness.

It is one that breeds selfishness and pride and contention. This is not the way of the Lord. Nowhere in the definition of love, is kindness, meekness and selflessness there room for the aforementioned attributes. Christ gave all that He had, including His life for the benefit of others.

The message of the Gospel was his ultimate answer to wealth, and Jesus said unto them, *I am the bread of life; he that cometh to me shall never hunger and he that believeth on me shall never thrust.* [192] What greater wealth could one desire but to never be hungry or thirsty again? Truly, with the Gospel in your life…you need nothing else!

---

[192] Jhn 6:35

Epilogue:

I was first inspired to write this book years ago when I received the personal revelation on marriage, chapter 15, The New and Everlasting Covenant while atop Mt Phillips, New Mexico. I was impressed that the message was "bigger than me" and surely had a greater audience than "just for me." As the years have passed and I have thwarted death so many times, it reinforced the impression that I have been preserved for a greater purpose than just to keep my seemingly meaningless existence intact.

I therefore embarked on the task to put these impressions and thoughts to text so that my purpose may be fulfilled. It has taken years of my life and countless emotional reflections to complete the work. I have never enjoyed reading anything I did not have to nor felt that I could equate to any competency as a writer, of which by now you may surely agree. It was only my desire to do what the Lord wanted.

As a result, I carefully prepared the material for commercial publication which was expectantly denied at every turn. Fulfilling the message contained in Chapter 20, _Your Destination May Not be Your Objective,_ the Lord has once again taught me a lesson. When contemplating the purpose of this material and realizing that no broader interest occurred, an impression came to me similar to so many I have received before........... "If you knew that there was no broader audience, you would have never written it." The Lord only told me what I needed to know to get the job done. I was the one that made the assumptions as to why. This is how the Lord has often dealt with me. He knows of my indifference, impatience and pessimism. The purpose of this book is now clear, the "broader audience" I seek are those of my immediate family and their prosperity or as the Lord has otherwise intended of which I have no knowledge or control.

Mine may be just another name on the lines of the generational charts to my descendants but the material in this book will bring life to the otherwise faceless name. Hopefully, meaning and direction will be given to its reader for some purpose only known by the Lord Himself

This is now my purpose and meaning, to help others along the path of life as the Lord directs. Keep the faith, don't ever give up and keep fighting until you hear the words, "well done, thou good and faithful servant."[193]

Until we meet again................Pops.

---

[193] Matthew 25:21

Made in the USA
Columbia, SC
09 October 2023

24171747R00187